STARTUP
SCALEUP
OR
SCREWUP

Why businesses fail to
scale and how to fix it

TOM WILLIAMS
FIVE-TIME BUSINESS FOUNDER

Rethink

First published in Great Britain in 2023 by Rethink Press
(www.rethinkpress.com)

Contents

Introduction

If you want to make a difference, make a fortune and make it fun while you're doing it, nothing can match building your own business.

Having founded five diverse businesses myself, and since working with many founders as a business coach, I've seen the power a successful business can have to transform the lives of its owners. If it's a good business, it can make a difference to the lives of customers, employees and even the community as well.

Small business owners employ the majority of people in the private sector in Australia,[1] and many other countries in the Western world. For employees, a growing business provides not just security but also the prospect of advancing their skills and career path.

For the founders, it's their chance to write their own history, to blaze their own trail by creating a company in their image, which expresses their values.

Running your own growing business means you can be the designer of your life. You can decide who you want to serve and how you want to do it. You get the satisfaction of seeing the impact you have on other people's lives. If things are going well, you will also be making considerably more money than you would ever make working for other people.

This book is intended as a guide for small business owners who start their businesses as experts or specialists in a particular area. Perhaps you've been working as an accountant for a large company and one day you think, 'I can do better starting my own accounting business.' Or you might be an engineer, a designer, a baker, an IT expert or a town planner. Whatever the area, you set out to build your own business with the expectation that you'll make more money and have more time for yourself and your family.

Often things start out pretty well, given you have expertise, enthusiasm and put in the hard yards to provide a good service or build a good product. However, after a few years, you may find you're working longer hours than you ever did before and the wage you take home, after paying staff and overheads, is actually less than you'd earn as an expert working for others.

Getting your staff to work together harmoniously and take ownership for the whole company's future seems out of reach. Despite your best efforts, they don't seem to operate by the values you'd expect. Your customers are late with their payments and the bank won't extend your overdraft. Your sales growth has slowed to a crawl and your partner is complaining you never have time for the family. What started out as a glorious dream has become a stress-filled round of Groundhog Day hassles. Unless you can find a way out of this mess, you're at risk of burnout, or even of bankruptcy.

In 2021–22 in Australia, 35% of businesses failed after four years, which was an improvement from a 48% failure rate the year before. Survival rates are similar or worse in other countries, with 43% failing after four years in the US and 54% in the UK. Of those who survived, in Australia only 7% generated income above $2m a year.[2]

One reason even the business owners who survive struggle to grow past this level is because to go beyond it they must change the way they run their business. They may be world-class experts in their field of specialisation, but at a certain stage of growth they realise they're struggling to become an expert in business leadership and management. They may accept they need to move from working *in* the business to working *on* the business, but they're not sure how to do it. For years they've been 'the first violinist', but now they must become 'the conductor'.

Another reason for getting stuck at this stage is the struggle to give up being the guru, the go-to problem solver, the person everyone leans on for the answers. Business owners get a dopamine hit from being the supreme juggler, typically loving being the innovator, the salesperson or the guy who delivers the service. They won't hand over enough tasks to other people because they don't think they'd get them done as well as doing them themselves. They haven't built a system to ensure that they do get done – if not quite as well, at least to a satisfactory standard.

The typical complaint of business owners in this dilemma is that they just don't have enough hours in the day to do it all. Their problem is not time management, it's *focus* management. Learning what to focus on may not be obvious. Some people are born entrepreneurs, but for others, such as me, the journey of learning how to grow a business was anything but straightforward.

After graduating with a BSc with honours in pharmacology, I went to work as a research assistant at the Melbourne University Department of Medicine at Austin Hospital. I'd been offered the opportunity to do a PhD and continue the research. It was important work and it should have been satisfying, but after a year something was wrong. I remember one day coming into the labs and looking around at other researchers poring over their instruments, taking in the lingering pungent organic chemical smell that never quite leaves a lab and thinking, 'They seem to love it, but this isn't it for me.' I just couldn't imagine myself there long term, being, as they say, 'a lab rat'. I knew I needed something else, but I didn't know what.

A little while later, I saw a job with a large British pharmaceutical company, GSK, and got it. There, after a while, I 'jumped the fence' from science to business.

GSK initially put me to work writing applications for new drugs to the TGA, Australia's equivalent of the FDA. About six months later, they asked me to sit on their marketing and advertising committee to check their scientific accuracy. That began a serendipitous journey that led to a career in entrepreneurship and innovation. I soon discovered, as we sat around the table discussing how to market new products, that I had a stream of suggestions to contribute.

My ideas weren't based on any experience; rather it seemed I had bumped into a natural talent that had lain unnoticed during years of study in other areas. That led me to take on the role of launching a new GSK medicine for asthmatics in a new way. Instead of having the less-informed sales reps tell the complicated story of the drug's development and testing, I realised it would be better to have a world-class expert tell the story on video. The sales reps could then use the newly available medium of video cassettes to travel around the country showing the story to GPs.

It worked. In fact, it worked so well that it soon became the standard way GSK introduced new medicines in Australia. After a while, it was picked up and copied by other companies. I had changed the way marketing was done for an industry, just by asking how to do it better than the existing 'best practice'. Later, I used this same way of thinking to create game-changing innovations in other industries, including air travel, investment management and training for biomed scientists.

Most companies strive to meet best practice, but break-throughs come from seeing the limitations of best practice and exploring how else to achieve a higher goal.

At twenty-five, I thought making videos looked like more fun than anything else I'd done before, so to the shock of my boss and my parents, I abandoned my expected career path and joined up with a neighbour with film experience to start a video production company. We were making videos and integrating them with film and large-screen slide shows to launch new products for major companies like Holden, Ford, Qantas, Yamaha and Dunlop. Our shows travelled around Australia, within events we also co-ordinated, to introduce new products and services to the trade and the press.

This was my introduction to entrepreneurship. To the thrills and the spills of starting a business, seeing it become a living growing organism and attempting to understand how to make it better. Better for customers, better for employees, better for shareholders and better for the founders.

Over several decades I would become the founder or co-founder of five companies in diverse fields. There were some successes, with some exits, such as selling an investment management company to a global merchant bank, HSBC, and taking a biotech from Startup to a public listing on the Australian Stock Exchange. There were also some screwups, from which I probably learnt more. When things have been successful, you may not realise what was fundamental to that success, but when things fail, it's painfully obvious what went wrong.

By reading this book you'll understand how to install the essential foundations and springboards for sustainable growth. You'll see where you are on the roadmap, where you might be bumping up into a growth ceiling and what to do to break through. It won't be by working *harder*, but rather by working *smarter* to steadily build the strategy, the team and the systems for the whole business. Instead of spinning your wheels, you'll be spending your time on things that move the needle. With persistence and some disciplined focus, you'll achieve your well-defined purpose for a well-defined niche of ideal clients, delivering a well-defined outcome.

It took me many years, working on my own businesses and drawing on my roots as a scientist, searching for the formula for succeeding in business, tracking down what worked and why. Gradually – too gradually for my liking – I came to realise there were five essential pillars that a company has to get right. Without considerable refinement in these five areas, it is impossible to grow in a sustainable – let alone rapid – way. With them, it's almost like having springboards that launch you into the next phase of growth. As a bonus, with these platforms in place you'll find more time for yourself and your family, and with less stress you can finally enjoy the epic adventure of life as an entrepreneur.

I suppose you could say I've been there and done that, spending forty years in a number of different businesses: five of my own, as well as positions in two global giants. I've developed a number of innovations within these different industries. I've also worked as a fund manager, assessing listed companies and working out in which ones to invest over $2 billion of superannuation fund money.

This combination has given me an unusual breadth of experience, which in conjunction with experience coaching other businesses, has helped me to crystallise a formula for more growth with less stress. It's based on five essential springboards that empower business owners who've come from an expert background, to make the shift from operators to leaders who can break through their company's growth ceilings, with only minor screwups en route.

You can read this book from start to finish, or if you have a burning issue on your mind, you can jump to the relevant chapter, check out the summary and go from there. Sometimes it's better to start at the end; however, I do suggest you at least read the first two chapters on the stages of growth initially, as they will provide the foundation for the rest of the material.

In writing this book and laying out these five essential springboards, my wish is that you'll learn how to do it all more quickly and easily than I did. In the process, make a difference and have some fun while you're making a fortune.

The stages of business growth

In 1922, Niels Bohr won the Nobel prize for his shell model of the atom, which explained how electrons didn't drift from one orbit to another but rather they jumped in discrete steps.[3] He went on to show that when they jumped to a lower orbit they emitted a fixed quanta of energy as radiation, and in order to jump to a larger orbit, they needed to absorb a fixed quantum of energy.

I think growing businesses also change from one state to another in discrete steps that require certain inputs at certain stages. A change in focus, energy and activity is needed to get through these stage gates and move into the next phase.

In science, you start off with an hypothesis and then look at the evidence to see if it fits to confirm or disprove your theory. What follows is my hypothesis of how businesses move from one stage to another and what 'energy' in the form of management's focus and actions is needed to make the leaps. I'm setting out to explain why some businesses get stuck below a growth ceiling and struggle to break through it.

Businesses go through stages of growth that do not respond to simply more of what was done before. While the stage gates vary somewhat according to the type of business, for most that I've observed, the stages and their approximate annual gross income levels look like this.

1. Setup $0 to $300,000

2. Startup $300,000 to $1m

3. Stepup $1m to $4m

4. Scaleup $4m to $10m

5. Grownup $10m plus

The stages that many expert founders get stuck at are the leap from Startup to Stepup and from Stepup to Scaleup.

This book focuses on the five essential springboards needed to get past these gates:

1. Proposition	Nail the value proposition
2. Planning	Design from the future, looking back
3. People	Build a team that takes total ownership
4. Process	Make it all work together
5. Promotion	Create an ongoing marketing and sales machine

By understanding in some depth what's required in each of these essential areas, a founder can make the shift from expert to entrepreneur, from operator to owner. They will learn to become the leader of a team that takes total ownership of the challenge of achieving the company mission. Businesses that work towards mastering these five springboards will move through the stage gates and keep growing.

I should say, however, that the definition of some of these terms varies with different people and contexts. Steve Jobs considered Apple was still a Startup because he wanted to retain the inventiveness and agility of the Silicon Valley mindset he and Steve Wozniak had when they began. By some people's definition, a company can only be called a Scaleup if it can be duplicated many times over, like McDonald's restaurants, or scaled to be used by people all over the planet, like Google.

If you have a business that can become an Apple, a McDonalds or a Google, that's great. You probably don't need this book. On your way out the door, kindly send me a prospectus to buy some of your shares.

If, on the other hand, you merely want to grow your business tenfold, make a pile of money, make a difference to your customers and employees, get some time back to spend with your family, reduce your stress levels, grow your skills as an entrepreneur and enjoy one of life's great adventures, read on.

1
Quantum Shifts

Setup stage – below $300,000 per annum

Many people will include this as part of the Startup stage, but to my mind it's a separate precursor. Here, the founder has the challenge of discovering if they have a viable business concept.

The founder may have seen a market opportunity or recognised a problem he or she thinks they can solve, or they may simply be following a passion to see if they can make it into a business. This is the inspiration stage.

Design thinking principles would recommend that the founder first seeks an in-depth understanding of the intended customer issues before they rush to find a solution. However, it's often the case that founders fall in love with their ideas and don't stop to test their assumptions. They are so passionate about their baby, they blindly race to get it produced and launched. I call it the entrepreneur's trap and I've done it myself.

> Sometimes businesses fail because they run out of money. More often, it's because they produce something nobody wants – or at least they don't want it badly enough to buy it in sufficient numbers. Other times it's because the idea is ahead of its time or launched ahead of the technology that would make it a success.

A decade before the launch of the smartphone, I was introduced to someone with a neat creation: a pocket guidebook to London with the essentials of finding cafes, hotels, attractions and transport, all colour-coded and cross-referenced into a pull-out map. It made finding your way around London ridiculously easy for the first-time visitor. To make it even more usable, the pull-out map had ingeniously enlarged the central tourist areas and diminished the surrounding areas, while keeping them in view. I loved this rough version and agreed to form a company to professionally design, produce and sell it. It was called the *London Locator*.

I knew one of Australia's best graphic designers, so we had the *London Locator* designed and then got

10,000 copies printed. I negotiated a distribution deal in Australia and London, and we thought we would be off and running with plans to do similar versions for Paris and New York.

We did sell the 10,000 books with a lot of hard slog over a year, but repeat orders were not coming in from the bookshops. Why?

We knew from feedback that customers who used it loved it and found it just what they needed for their first few days in a strange city. However, further interviews with bookstore managers suggested we lacked 'shelf appeal'. It seemed people coming in looking for books on London were either looking for glossy photo-packed books with architectural cutaways, or the kind of insiders' stories of secret haunts to explore in the back streets. Our little book, though fulfilling a 'need', did not fulfil a 'want' – or at least not one people had in mind walking into a bookshop.

I had another bright idea – or so I thought – about how to sell it. Why don't we pitch it to Qantas or British Airways to give to passengers on their way to London? But to my dismay, when we did manage to get meetings, we were told they expected to get things like this for free. Perhaps we could have sought advertisers to subsidise costs to make the book free, but energy and finances were diminishing by that stage, so sadly we closed the *London Locator* down. Had we started a decade later, it probably would have made a great app for the iPhone, which could have been regularly updated and refined.

In the Italian crime drama *Ice Cold Murders*, a cranky unorthodox detective, Rocco Schiavone, arrives in the alpine town of Valle d'Aosta, having been posted from Rome over his disregard for rules. There he and his somewhat hapless team find various troubles, which he labels according to his internal assessment of how much of a 'pain in the arse' they are.[4] Following his guide, I'll label the *London Locator* result as a level seven pain, or screwup. It would have rated higher, but for the valuable, albeit painful, lessons I learnt.

Testing

You've probably heard the expression, 'Build it and they will come.' What you should be thinking, however, is: 'If they come, I will build it.' Test the waters to see if your great idea is something people want to buy before committing the big bucks to produce and launch it.

The focus in the Setup stage is on exploration. The priorities are to create the first iterations of the product – the so-called minimal viable product (MVP) – and test its appeal with groups of potential customers. The step we missed, resulting in the *London Locator* screwup, was showing a mock-up to a handful of bookshops to get their feedback on its appeal and likelihood of success. You need to find out what potential customers, or people with intimate understanding of customers, think of it. Will they happily pay to solve their problems or quench their desires at a price and volume to provide sufficient income for your fledgling new business to survive?

The founder may have a plan, but no battle plan survives first contact with the enemy and no early business plan survives first contact with the customers. As Mike Tyson put it, 'everyone has a plan until they get punched in the mouth',[5] and to the committed entrepreneur who has their heart set on their baby, negative feedback does feel like a punch in the mouth.

The trick is to learn to welcome critical feedback, listen with an open mind to what they say and dig a little more. Ask your audience what their frustrations are, what they want that isn't already available and what's important to them. Instead of starting with your idea or product, look with a blank sheet for what would be a game changer to solve their burning problems or meet their deepest desires. This can then open up better opportunities to make and sell something a customer really wants.

The founder must be a visionary but also a Jack or Jill of all trades. They will be doing or overseeing the product development, customer conversations and sales, delivery of the product or service and the accounting (or at least supervising invoicing and payments). They will also be setting up a website, marketing, thinking about first employees, worrying about finding the right people and managing them. On and on it goes.

The Setup stage is about finding out if your product or services meet these three criteria:

- Is it desirable, meaning it meets an existing primary human desire?
- Is it feasible, meaning it can be made and delivered?
- Is it viable, meaning the financial returns are sufficient to continue in business?

If you can answer yes to all three, and you have sufficient bootstrap funding to get going, you can pass through the gateway to the next stage.

Most businesses will make a loss when they start out, so the initial challenge is to find the first few paying customers, learn from their feedback and get the business moving forward. For self-funded – or so-called bootstrapped – businesses, the Setup stage usually covers businesses from initial concept through break even and up to around $300,000 revenue per year.

The pitch

If you need funding, the challenge before launch is to find the right investors and pitch it to them. If that is your situation, then, like many other steps in business, the first thing to do is to understand what's going on in the minds of your audience. Your investor could be one of the following:

- Family and friends   Usually approached for funds under $50,000
- Angel investors   For funds up to $500,000
- Venture capital (VC)   For funds up to $5m in seed rounds

A good pitch must understand what the prospective investor is looking for and their already existing beliefs and criteria. Angel investors want to make money but are generally also motivated to help entrepreneurs who work in an area they care about. They will often be happy to mentor the founders, or at least provide suggestions based on their own experience, as the business gets set up.

VCs are a rather different proposition. They are looking for investments that can make a ten-fold or twenty-fold return on their investment, in part because they know that out of a typical portfolio of seven to ten investments, about six will be duds, two will be OK and, at best, two will be 'home runs'. At the time of deciding to invest, they must believe yours will be a home run.

They are also looking for investments with an exit plan; usually either a trade sale to a larger company or an IPO (initial public offering) on a stock market like the

ASX or Nasdaq. They are usually working on a seven-to ten-year timeline to make a series of investments and then exit them, in order to return funds to the groups like the superannuation funds that they raised the money from in the first place. As the founder, you may or may not want to sell out of your company, so you need to take this into account, but if you want VC money they will insist on an exit plan for their proportion at least. Most of the time this plan works for them and their investors, but how would you feel if you had sold out of Apple or Google after just a few years?

There is also the matter of market size to consider. You might have plans for a good little business, but if it's not groundbreaking and addressing a large global market, then VCs are probably not interested.

Your pitch deck

In any case, you are probably going to need a pitch deck (in other words, a slide presentation). Here are the typical components:

1. A title, logo and phrase that sums up your business or its promise to customers.

2. A summary of the business vision and the funds sought, known as 'the ask'.

3. The problem or desire: why it's significant, yet unsolved.

4. The size of the market for existing solutions.

5. Your ideal customer and the size of your initial niche target market.

6. Your competitive advantage.

7. Your team, their experience and roles.

8. The milestones and path to market.

9. Financial forecasts to show the return on investment.

10. The ask, in detail. How much you want in return for what share of the company.

11. The exit plan, if pitching to VCs.

12. A summary of this great opportunity.

I suggest preparing a short, intermediate and fully detailed longer version. You never know when you might need each one.

When I was CEO of a biotech company, we'd begun talking to a potential investor in Hong Kong to invest up to $3m. After some initial conversations, he invited me over to visit him and pitch. As this was a big deal for our fledgling company, I prepared a long, detailed slide presentation and flew over.

On the first day, expecting to meet him, I got a message that something had come up and we would have to wait until tomorrow. 'Fine,' I thought as I polished up and added even more to the slide presentation in my hotel room. The next day, another message and another delay.

Now, of course, my mind started to worry, but still I reasoned things would be fine. The third day came and I got a message saying to meet him and some friends for a casual dinner that night and he would finally make time the day after that to listen to my formal pitch.

So, I rolled up to the dinner and was ushered into a private dining room at the top of a hotel with sweeping views over the harbour lights. There were about eight people there and we proceeded to have drinks. I intermittently joined in the conversations between what were obviously close colleagues, who discussed everything, but nothing to do with our biotech business.

Suddenly after entrées, the potential investor turned to me and said, 'I'm sorry Tom, but I can't see you tomorrow and I have to fly overseas after that. But we have a few minutes before the main course now, so tell us about your business and why I should invest.'

After choking on my last mouthful of the entrée, and instantly regretting having started on my second glass of the Grand Cru French Bordeaux that the investor's wife had brought to the dinner, I launched into an off-the-cuff account of the product and business, while trying to remember all the great stuff sitting in the slide deck back in my hotel room.

They expressed polite interest and asked a couple of questions, but soon the main course arrived, and the conversation switched back to holidays, family and the Hong Kong economy. I thought to myself, 'Well that was a level eight screwup,' To my surprise, a few weeks later we got the $3m.

The main things needed to make the jump to the next stage from here:

- A complete and remarkable solution – one so much better than existing alternatives that people naturally want to tell their friends about it.

- Some not-too-terrible marketing, to launch it and raise awareness it exists.

Startup stage – $300,000 to $1m

This is the stage where you have your business up and running. If you've nailed your value proposition, demand is growing to the point where you're struggling to keep up. Now you need to add capacity to keep growing.

While the financial divisions between stages are somewhat flexible, companies in this stage typically have income between $300,000 and $1m a year.

At this stage you're turning your attention to building a real business with the following core components:

- Product or service development
- Marketing

- Sales

- Product or service delivery

- Financial accounts

- Back-office admin

Most founders go into business with expertise in a domain. For example, when I co-founded the audio-visual production company, my partner brought with him existing expertise in film production. That was where his training had been and that formed the basis of the capability of our company to make audiovisual programmes for companies. A plumber might expand from providing plumbing services to hiring other plumbers or sourcing a range of taps and other plumbing-related products to distribute. An accountant might partner with a lawyer to set up a combined service and co-working space for entrepreneurs. A graphic designer might start a digital marketing agency.

In other words, most businesses are set up by people with technical expertise, rather than expertise in running a business, per se. However, as they begin to grow and have more success, they rapidly need to become businessmen and businesswomen. They soon find they are having to learn about and deal with a lot of things out of their initial area of expertise – things like recruiting and employment law, cash flow forecasts, marketing funnels, computer software systems and so on.

They often get stuck under a growth ceiling below $1m in revenue because they are struggling to shift from working *in* the business, as the expert, to working *on* the business, as the CEO.

They don't have the experience or skills to hire the best people for key roles and they don't know how to manage them, or what to do if they're not performing up to expectations. They don't have the experience or skills to set up management accounts for financial insight and control. They don't have a pathway mapped out to find new customers and take them on a journey from awareness, through several steps to build trust and show value, on to sales.

This stage can feel overwhelming like you're on a never-ending treadmill run. No matter how fast you run, you feel like the legend of Sisyphus, pushing a large stone up a hill each day, only for it to roll down the hill again each night.

This is the stage where business owners feel like they just need more time to get it all done. In reality, they need to spend their time on different things.

The main focus points needed to make the jump to the Stepup stage from here:

- A shift from expert to entrepreneur.
- Defining your mission and the strategy to achieve it.

- Building a good team with the right people in key roles.

- Beginning to set up systems in key areas.

- Refining the value proposition if needed and turning marketing and sales into a measurable procedure.

Stepup stage – $1m to $4m

Now the business starts to gain momentum and break through growth ceilings. The business begins to become known and develop a reputation, even the beginnings of a brand. You no longer have to chase every customer; they are starting to come to you. Businesses in this phase are earning between $1m and $4m per annum.

You have your product or service sorted out and you're getting excellent feedback from customers regarding their satisfaction with your product and service.

You're setting budgets, and your team is tracking and mostly achieving them. You're refining your measurement of progress in financial matters and in other areas. You're flat-out satisfying demand, but the business has a lighter feel to it than in the Startup stage. People want to come to work in your business and there's a buzz about the place.

You're employing more people on a regular basis and it becomes a key challenge to find and retain the right people. By now you may have a bonus arrangement and perhaps an employee stock ownership plan (ESOP) in place.

> The fly by the seat of your pants, gonzo hustle, 'make it happen and clean up the mess later' approach that was necessary to get off the ground needs to shift to a more professional 'do it by the book' method. Your problems centre around getting and keeping the right people and having them behave as a high-performing co-operative team. It's time to design how you want the business to look for the longer term and make plans for expansion.

When business owners reach this stage, they assume they're going to keep growing and are surprised to find they can get stuck under about $4m in turnover. The sticking points revolve around first of all shifting what the owner is spending their time on, so they are ahead of the game, thinking strategically instead of running after the daily urgencies. To become an effective CEO, they need to give away a large part of being the expert, at least being the operating expert, even if they remain the standard bearer. An executive assistant may be needed, and a general manager, if they are to break free of the whirlwind and spend their time building the brand to an external audience. They need to refine their systems and probably upgrade the software to run them. A governance process will need setting up, perhaps with a quarterly financial and operational report to an advisory board, coach or mentor. They must get a team in place that lives the values and standards of behaviour the owner would like to have them operate by. Quite often this doesn't happen by instinct and needs a lot of engagement, buy-in and accountability to achieve. Otherwise, the owner can get frustrated and, over time, disheartened or even burned out. Sometimes the founder's daily diligence is the problem; if they stepped back or took a prolonged holiday, it would allow space for others to step up and take responsibility. Instead of shifting existing people around to find a role they can do properly, the owner must make the role requirements the guiding force and, if necessary, look outside to fill them.

The main things needed to make the jump to the Scaleup stage from here:

- A shift from operator to leader.

- Identifying your ideal clients and saying no to others.

- Defining roles and responsibilities, finding department heads that take ownership for leading a functional team. Rating performance, training for improvement, or – where unproductive – for departure.

- Refining operational procedures and systems, so consistent results are assured.

- Creating a repeatable, reliable marketing and sales process.

- Total commitment to making targets, tracking performance as a team, with individual and group accountability.

- Taking care of team mental well-being, while insisting on them maintaining the values, standards and code of conduct for their culture.

Scaleup stage – $4m to $10m

By now you have a well-defined marketing and sales pipeline. You know how to reach your ideal customers and the pitch to get them beginning the journey through multiple touch points to a sales conversation. You can measure the conversion at each stage, and you know your return on investment. Now you have a profit centre instead of a cost. Businesses in this stage are typically earning between $4m and $10m.

At this stage, you need to cement your brand and its positioning in your industry. Preferably you'll build a brand that customers so want, they are happy to pay a premium for it, thereby creating intrinsic value and greater profit margins. If, on the other hand, your game is to be the cheapest provider of a commodity-like product, range of products or services, then you need to create an efficient low-cost operating model or some non-financial intrinsic value, such as being a one-stop shop where they can get everything.

JB Hi-Fi started in 1974 with a single store in Keilor, Melbourne. Its philosophy of providing trending entertainment products at discount prices, with knowledgeable friendly service in a store that deliberately looks like a jumble sale, remains a successful model today, after growing to over 200 stores and withstanding the arrival of online rivals like Amazon.[6]

In the Scaleup stage, your focus needs to be on culture, on building leaders and a team that works beyond any silos to take ownership for the success of the whole enterprise. By now you'll have moved from an advisory board to a more formal board, assessing performance and decisions every month. You'll be taking on new avenues for growth, such as mergers and acquisitions, or moving into new markets with extensions or total innovations.

The main things needed to make the jump to the Grownup stage from here:

- A shift from working on what now to working on what's next.

- A customer-focused culture that picks up market shifts.

- Building the next level of leaders in the organisation.

- Becoming the employer of choice in your niche.

- A relentless focus on refining systems for operational excellence.

- New avenues of growth.

- Expressing the brand as a category leader.

Grownup stage – beyond $10m

To move into real maturity as a business, you need to make explicit what used to be implicit: procedures, systems, communication and accountability. You probably have more people than you can personally speak to on a regular and frequent basis, so you must create ways to keep the communication flowing, and build the engagement and the sense of belonging in a larger group of people, who may now be working at several different sites.

By now you must have capable leaders heading key departments. Once you do have them, the job of being the CEO actually becomes easier than at the previous stage, as now you have a group of other people solving problems and making decisions without your constant input.

Your company might have initially won a lot of business because of your expertise and creativity – your 'edge'. Now, as you chase larger customers, you'll find they want more than that. Big organisations want to know you can provide a complete, end-to-end service, and have the deep capacity to handle all aspects of their size of business. There's a never-ending cycle of improving systems and professionalism in all areas.

Even at this stage, in service businesses, many customers will have come to do business with an individual, rather than the company. One of the challenges now is to build the brand beyond that, so customers come to do business with the company and accept whoever the company recommends they deal with. It's time for the founder to set up a succession plan, so the organisation can live on without them, even if they remain in the business for some years to come.

Investors or other companies will probably be making offers to buy into the business, or buy the business outright, so the owners need to consider their long-term plans. It might be time to consider a public listing on the Australian or another stock exchange, to raise capital for another leap forward.

There'll likely be a need for larger investment in continuous innovation to compete with other companies eyeing off your success and wanting a piece of it. You may need to decide what your next big thing is and form a separate division to develop and launch it. As disruptive technology changes come along through you or others, keep in mind the business you're in, so you don't say no to opportunities that may look different, but still serve the underlying desires of your customers.

You need a positive reinforcing cycle of activities that build on each other to create more customers and deliver more value, which then delivers more customers and more profit.

As the business leader, you'll need to increasingly be spending your time on the long-term future, thinking about industry changes, strategies for growth, external stakeholders and culture.

Setup	Explore options to find first customers Test product/services and refine
Startup	Nail value proposition Hire key people & hold accountable Develop strategic plan
Stepup	Set up systems/stop founder doing it all Optimise marketing & sales Develop culture & team performance
Scaleup	Develop leaders Measure operational excellence Build a brand
Grownup	Find additional growth Set up business for life after founder Look further into the future

Focus points for growing beyond different stages

2

The Five Springboards

There are five main areas of focus for an entrepreneur to think through, articulate and act on to make the leap from one stage to the next and keep growing in a sustainable way.

I call these areas springboards because, with them in place, it becomes possible to make these leaps a little easier and with less stress. And while you will revisit and adjust these elements as you bust through your stage gates onto the next stage, it's surprising how much remains the same once you have them right.

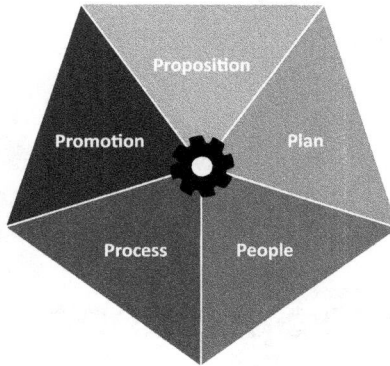

The five essential springboards, empowering growth

1. Proposition

Every company that's growing strongly has a compelling value proposition, meaning what it is your customers value so highly they're eager to buy it. Every company that isn't growing hasn't nailed this yet. If demand isn't exceeding your capacity to supply, you need to do more work on the product, service and value proposition.

Most of this challenge is understanding what your customers really need and want, and providing it with your existing or, if necessary, new products and services.

If you have a great proposition that your customers value highly and a halfway reasonable method of promoting your products or services, then you're ready to bust through your growth ceilings and scale. You have the sales and potential to take on more staff and put in the systems to continue the growth of your business.

This section will walk you through what a great value proposition looks like and how to create one for your business.

2. Plan

Every business needs a game plan – one based on their purpose – and the strategy to fulfil it. The first steps are creative and exploratory. Once they're in place, the focus shifts to excellence in execution.

A good plan sets your direction and foundations for the long term and makes it easy to decide what to do in the short term. While some aspects change and adapt, the core will remain your guiding star.

This section will help you define your true north, develop a road map to get there and then measure progress en route.

3. People

When you have the right people in the right roles on your team and they are actually playing like a team, business becomes a lot easier and more enjoyable. When you don't, it can be hell.

Understanding your natural talents and how you can become the leader you need to be will help you make the shift from expert to entrepreneur, from operator to leader. As your business grows, developing the culture within your organisation becomes more important for both performance and satisfaction at work.

This section will help you hire the right people suited to their roles, stimulate engagement and teamwork, and become an employer of choice.

4. Process

Developing systems in the key areas of your business is necessary for sustainable, scalable growth.

Once you have a process down in a form that's understood by all and can be taught to new employees, the reliability of delivering good outcomes increases and life at work becomes less stressful.

This section will show you how to map out and refine processes to get the improvements in outcomes that will allow you to expand your staff and scale your business.

5. Promotion

If you don't have a repeatable and reliable way of getting new customers, you don't really have a business that can be scaled.

How you make people aware of what you offer and take them on a journey to becoming customers is changing with new technology and social media. The core principles of developing a brand for a tribe of eager customers remains the same.

This section will help you to understand and create a marketing machine that can bring you the right kind of prospects and convert them over time to long-lasting customers that become advocates for your company.

SPRINGBOARD 1
PROPOSITION

Nail the value proposition

The next time you buy or admire a piece of gold jewellery, stop for a moment to think of the amazing journey the raw material has been on to get to you.

When a massive star collapses it sometimes forms a super-energetic supernova, known as a magnetorotational hypernova.[7] Dr Chiaki Kobayashi and her all-female team used the Sky Mapper Telescope in Australia to discover a star like this, twenty-five times more massive than the Sun, on the edge of the Milky Way. An estimated 13 billion years ago, this explosive event led to a process called rapid neutron capture, resulting in the formation of all the heavy metals, including gold, that found their way to Earth.[8] In

1969, some of that settled star dust left Earth again, when gold was used as a thin thermonuclear protective coating on the face shields of the first astronauts to land on the Moon.[9]

Gold has been a source of fascination for thousands of years, for its beauty and extraordinary properties and as a store of value. When gold was discovered in California and Australia in the early 1850s, it led to the mass arrivals of migrants hoping to strike it rich.[10] My great-great-grandfather walked – yes, walked – from Adelaide to the Ballarat diggings and back twice to try his luck. He didn't find gold, but he realised those who did needed somewhere to keep it, so he began to manufacture tamper-proof safes. Alfred Simpson had an eye for what people needed. He went on to use the tinsmithing skills he'd learnt as a teenager in England to make pots and pans, bedsteads and colonial stoves. He set up early sheetmetal works in Adelaide, that grew over several generations into Simpsons white-goods, best known in later years for their washing machines.

Business at its essence is an exchange of value. As a seller, your job is to create something people will value highly enough to exchange gold, money, or something you want, in return.

What do we value? In 1943, American psychologist Abraham Maslow published a paper entitled, 'A Theory of Human Motivation'.[11] In his paper, he proposed a hierarchy of needs, whereby the lower order of needs take precedence over higher-order needs. Although his original proposal has been criticised for a lack of extensive proof, or cultural differences, it's nevertheless self-evident that if your survival is threatened, you tend to address that first.

Mind you, I have seen TV antennas on some of the poorest dwellings on Earth. Our assumptions of what our customers value the most warrant more than a superficial examination.

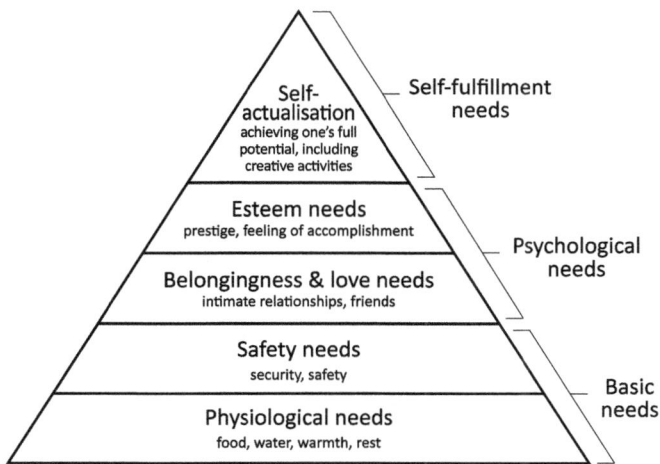

Maslow's hierarchy of needs

3

What Business Are You In?

John Russell, the former managing director of Harley-Davidson Europe, was once asked by a journalist, 'How's the motorcycle business going?'

John replied, 'I don't know, we're not in the motorcycle business.'

Puzzled, the journalist asked, 'Well what business are you in? Don't you sell motorbikes?'

He replied, 'Harley-Davidson sells 43-year-old accountants the ability to dress in black leather, ride through small towns and have people be afraid of them.'[12]

Harley-Davidson sells a dream – you might say part of the American Dream – of being a bit of a rebel who can do whatever he damn well wants. The motorcycle is merely a means to achieve that feeling.

People buy products or services to get an outcome. As Harvard marketing professor Theodore Levitt famously put it, 'People don't buy a quarter-inch drill, they buy a quarter-inch hole.'[13]

The outcome can be functional, financial, emotional or social – or quite often it's a mixture of several of these. To continue with the drill example, the functional outcome would be to make a hole in the wall to hang a picture, and the financial outcome desired might be to do it for the lowest cost. Alternatively, you may want to enhance your self-image of being a handyman or boast a little to the neighbours. In this case you might be willing to buy a more expensive drill, or a drill kit with other attachments, to hang on your garage wall. Different drill makers have assessed their capabilities, identified a market niche, and produced products that make different promises or value propositions.

If you've done a good job of this, you can withstand a lot of competition. When Japan introduced its motorbikes to America, they were cheaper, faster and more reliable than Harley-Davidson. Because they had a clear insight into the business they were really in, Harley-Davidson didn't chase what Japanese motorbikes offered.[14] They were loyal to their customers' deepest wants, and in return retained a loyal niche of customers.

What feeling or emotionally important connection do you provide? You could say:

- Mortgage brokers are not just finding you a loan, they're in the business of delivering the Australian dream.

- Insurance companies are in the business of preventing panic attacks and giving you a good night's rest.

- Clothing stores are in the business of making you look like the person you'd like to become.

- Schools are in the business of putting old heads on young shoulders.

- Fine restaurants are in the business of providing exclusive experiences.

Now, your value proposition doesn't have to be anything like those. But it probably isn't what people – or perhaps even *you* – think of as the obvious one, based on your product or service. If you've misunderstood your value proposition, not only can it limit your growth but it can also put you out of business.

One of the jobs my partner and I had in the early days of our audiovisual production business was to launch a new camera for Kodak with a show for camera dealers and the press in Australia. The camera we were asked to launch was their first with self-developing film, intended to compete with Polaroid. We sent out an x-ray of the camera as an intriguing invitation and created a show with the aim of demonstrating that for Kodak, this was just another step in a long history of being at the forefront of changing ways of taking photos.

We concentrated on amateur family photos, where the framing might have chopped off part of a relative's head, or where an out-of-focus thumb intruded into the corner of the frame. Our show projected their history and their new camera, set to a poem we called, 'Ode to the humble snapshot.'

Some years later, their own scientists would create the first digital camera. But when the admittedly scratchy first version was presented to senior management, they rejected it because it didn't fit their concept of their value proposition and business model.

Kodak used to sell their cameras close to break even and make all their money on film, which they dominated worldwide. So, a camera that didn't need film was seen to be sabotaging their profitable business model. Whereas the founder George Eastman had twice in his lifetime abandoned current technology to take a leap of faith into a new way of taking pictures, this was too much for the professional management team that succeeded him.

Other companies took up and refined the digital camera and in 2012 Kodak filed for bankruptcy, as nobody was using film anymore.[15] Now, that was a level ten screwup.

What we had instinctively understood – but Kodak's management of the time didn't seem to – was that they weren't in the film business, per se. They were in the memory business.

Your definition of the business you're in should tap into the deeper emotional reason someone would want to buy your product or service. Do you know what that is for your business?

Big established businesses ought to know what business they're in. For small businesses, however, it's well worth exploring what business they *could* and *should* be in. Without that exploration, you may be limiting your growth potential by missing market segments you could serve well, or by failing to optimise what you offer to market segments you already serve.

It's useful to consider this with three parameters:

1. Your organisation's capabilities that are exceptional.

2. Market segments that have significant unsatisfied problems, or desires.

3. What functional and emotional outcome you could promise to deliver.

To consider fresh possibilities, ask yourself and your team these questions:

- What exceptional capabilities do we really have, whether currently in use or not?

- Which of our existing customers or market segments have a need for something beyond our current range of products or services?

- What new market segments have unsolved problems or desires, for which we could use our resources and capabilities to create solutions?

In each of these cases, what outcomes would we be promising those customers?

After this exercise, you should have a list of possibilities to consider and test.

Your ideal client

Your value proposition, like beauty, exists in the eye of the beholder. To understand what they consider a beautiful proposition requires understanding their persona in detail.

Start by thinking about a particular person and describing them to create an avatar. In this setting we are not talking about avatars as the material incarnation of deities, but rather a derivation from their more mundane use in computer games, as personalised illustrations of a user.

List the categories of work your business undertakes for clients. Rank them in order of financial value to you. Then for each category think of a typical customer for whom you do that kind of work or sell that kind of product. It helps to think of an actual person or two to base the exercise on. Give each one a name – even if you change it later – that sums them up in your mind, eg, Bob the builder or Sue the accountant. Fill out these kinds of details for each one to form your avatar.

Demographics

Is your ideal client a woman or man? What age are they? What level of education have they had? Are they 'self-made' or did they inherit money? What is their annual income?

What's their job and who do they work for? Where do they live; in what kind of home or rental accommodation? Are they married, with kids or not? What's their cultural background? What media do they look at and when?

Psychographics

What kind of lifestyle do they have? What are their interests, hobbies or sports? What are their politics, attitudes, opinions, beliefs and values? What are their

STARTUP, SCALEUP OR SCREWUP

personalities like? Are they risk takers or cautious? What's on their minds?

Your competitive advantage

What does your ideal client value most in doing business with you? Customers will have several criteria – either conscious or unconscious – for making purchasing decisions. Think about what they value the most. It could be a positive wish for something, it could be solving a pain point or fixing a frustration, or it could be a way of avoiding a risk.

These may include:

- Quality

- Range

- Ease of doing business

- Service

- Promptness

- Expertise

- Innovation

- Security

- Value for money

Rank four or five of these criteria in order of importance to your customer. If you know your customers well by all means do this exercise yourself, but it's useful to check later with some customers to validate your assumptions.

Compare how you rank (out of ten) with your three or four main competitors in a table.

Criteria	You	A	B	C
Expertise				
Ease				
Price				
Service				
Innovation				

*Competitive advantage ranked
by customer priorities*

Where do you have the strongest advantage? Where can you improve to compete more effectively in an area important to your customers? Where can you innovate or reposition to create a new benefit your competitors don't have?

Can you create an edge that others can't and defend it, with patents, secret know-how or formulas, trade secrets or the barriers to entry? In battle terms, can you build a moat to make your advantage sustainable?

CASE STUDY: P&B LAW

P&B Law is a St Kilda Road, Melbourne law firm, specialising in legal advice relating to property and business. Partners Jesse and Lindsay wanted to be sure they were providing and promoting what their clients valued most when choosing a particular law firm. First, we defined their different avatars in the categories of property, litigation, estate planning and commercial law. We described each avatar as you would knowing a real client.

Then we ranked what they and their senior team thought was of most value. They reasoned their potential clients would be looking for these characteristics:

1. Knowledgeable
2. Practical solutions
3. Responsive
4. Caring
5. Professional
6. Amicable relations
7. Hardworking

After marking, as fairly as they could, their level of service compared to their competitors, the team concluded they outshone the opposition in the areas of practical solutions and amicable relations, while matching the competition in the other areas.

Now they turned to test their own thinking against a group of potential clients.

Jesse and Lindsay were members of a peer advisory group of business leaders that I chaired under the auspices of The Executive Connection (TEC), who are part of the world's largest CEO network. They asked this group of founders and CEOs of businesses of the kind that would potentially use their services, what they most looked for in choosing a legal service, and this was what they said they wanted:

- Been there done that, depth of experience
- Give me the advice in three bullet points, free of legal jargon
- Trustworthy and accurate

They didn't care if their lawyer could tell them a joke. They didn't want to waste time or be charged for 'dad jokes'.

Getting honest feedback can be a little shocking, but it is extremely valuable. While it was helpful for workplace culture to crack a joke in the office, their clients wanted the benefit of their professional experience, delivered promptly, in clear terms they could easily understand.

The way Jesse and Lindsay summed it up after some further discussion with their internal team was, we're an experienced team providing clear advice you can trust to achieve your best outcome.

Your value proposition needs to be *their* value proposition.

Summary

- The business you're in is defined by the broad emotional desire you satisfy, which remains the same, even though technology, products and service details may change.

- Your ideal client avatar describes a realistic portrayal of one or more prototypical customers, including their demographic and psychographic profiles. Describing these details will help you think about the products or services they want and how to reach them.

- Your competitive advantage is whatever your clients value highly enough to make them bothered to switch over to you to obtain.

4

Expressing The Value Proposition

This is not something that you invent or manufacture a need for; it's an expression of a desire your customer already has that your product or service happens to fulfil. You might get lucky and find what you already have fits that need, but more likely you will have to create or modify your service or product to truly fulfil it.

For smaller businesses, nailing the value proposition is absolutely critical. In fact, if you're not growing at a rate that you're struggling to keep up with, it's likely to be because you haven't yet got a value proposition that has people queuing up to buy. Without this, it becomes almost impossible to scale – or at least generate – significant, sustainable annual growth rates.

The first *springboard* is getting a compelling value proposition. How do you do this? It has to be done by deep enquiry into your target customer's problems, their so-called pain points, or their desires, their wants. It's better if you can find a problem or desire that is a 'hair on fire' issue – in other words, they want a solution, now! That makes it a *need* to have rather than a *nice* to have.

Pippa and Hannah formed Merchgirls in 2015 with the aim of changing the promotional merchandise industry for the better.[16] They realised companies were getting frustrated with low-quality 'throw away' merchandise with unnecessary and problematic plastic wrapping. They set out to build a female-founded, design-led, sustainability-focused company, producing superior promotional merchandise that people would actually *want* to keep. That was their value proposition. The way they expressed it in their company tagline was, 'merchandise that's twice as nice'.

As awareness of environmental issues increased amongst Australian companies and as those companies saw something better was possible, Merchgirls found to their happiness that their better merch offering became a *need* to have, not just a *nice* to have service.

Here's a template for expressing your business value proposition:

List three or four frustra-tions, problems, burning desires of your customers	Across from them, list your solutions for each one

Now step back and look over what you've come up with. Work on summarising your solutions in a way that expresses how, as a whole, they comprehensively fix their issues. Initially do it in 'plain vanilla terms', without trying to be a copywriter, just yet.

A compelling value proposition ideally meets three criteria:

1. It's outcome specific: It spells out the specific benefits your target customer will receive.

2. It's pain focused: It states how your product fixes the customer's problem or improves their life.

3. It's exclusive: It highlights your competitive advantage and sets you apart from competitors.

If possible, make your value proposition specific. Instead of saying, 'Our scientific nutrition guide will help you lose weight,' say, 'Lose 6kg in 8 weeks with this weight loss programme designed by a professor of nutrition.' Once you have this, get creative, turning it into a punchy tagline or slogan.

Here are some examples from leading brands:[17]

Netflix value proposition: The biggest online subscription streaming service in the world.

Slogan: See what's next.

Nespresso value proposition: Enable consumers to easily make a variety of premium quality expresso coffee at home.

Slogan: A cup above.

Bunnings hardware value proposition: The largest range of hardware at the lowest prices, and if you can find something cheaper we'll beat it by 10%.

Slogan: Lowest prices are just the beginning.

Red Bull value proposition: A fashionable high energy drink that will help you perform at your youthful best.

Slogan: Red Bull gives you wings.

Secret sauce

If you look at how service companies market themselves, they pretty much all say they provide a high-quality service at a fair price with good, well-qualified staff. There's little or no differentiation to let potential customers know why they should pick them, rather than another.

People who have decided they need a particular service are looking for a reason to make a choice. If you can explain that you have a proprietary method, or special know-how, or a formula that's your IP, that will go a long way to providing the logical validation to choose your firm.

It's worth spending considerable time on this for your company, as it can clarify everything you're essentially setting out to achieve. If you've got it right, it can focus your marketing and build a following of loyal customers. If you realise you haven't got it right, it can usefully take you back to improving your product or service, to keep on improving it, to finally create something people will want so much they say, 'Shut up and take my money!'

Positioning

Another classical way of considering how you compare with competitors is to position your company and your competitors on a two-axis graph. This is an example for the car industry:

Let's say we plot the position of brands on the horizontal axis, from luxury to economy, and the brands on the vertical axis, from family cars at the bottom to performance cars at the top. We might put the Volkswagen Golf in the top-right quadrant with its combination of sportiness and economy. Mercedes is over on the left with luxury and family. Whereas Porsche would be near the edge of the quadrant with performance and luxury.

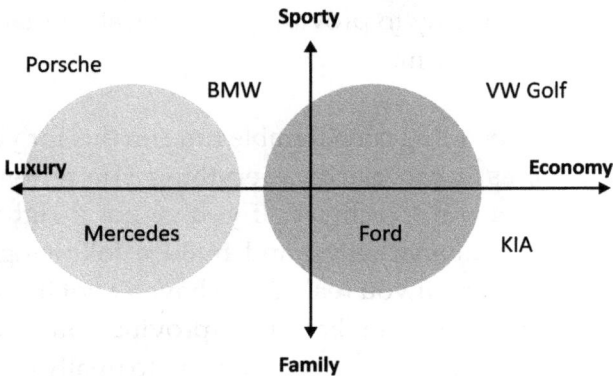

Sporty

Porsche

BMW   VW Golf

Luxury   Economy

Mercedes   Ford
                                    KIA

Family

Car market positioning

BMW would be sitting inside but lower in this quadrant, and you can go on to position other brands in economy and so on. Of course, large companies have quite a range of products with different characteristics, so they would occupy a larger shape on the grid. Other brands may attempt to spread their envelope, but can usually only do so within the limits of how customers perceive them.

The creative companies are those who can create a new category. The popularity of SUV probably started with the Range Rover, who created a new category with a vehicle that was luxurious, family orientated and could go off-road as well as on-road. Now Tesla has vehicles that are family sedans with the performance of top-of-the-line sports cars.

You can apply the same kind of analysis to any industry. Around the corner from where I live, there are six different cafes in the same street. Each one attempts to attract a slightly different audience. There's a French patisserie, a Greek deli where the focus is on takeaway food, an Australian cafe where the expresso machine is accessible from the street, an eat-in cafe with loud music and waiters serving a younger crowd, a fresh bread shop with coffee and a European-flavoured al fresco spot that took over from an Austrian-flavoured spot. While classical economics might forecast that the area was oversupplied and so demand should fall, for a while it seemed the more cafes there were, the more people arrived to partake.

Each cafe still needs to understand their audience and what they want. There used to be a cafe attempting a retro look with red-and-white-striped vinyl benches and a slim offering of Mediterranean meats on rotisseries to go with their coffee. This failed miserably since they didn't have a value proposition that drew enough customers, but the other cafes have each managed to find their position and thrive to varying degrees. Instead of a Starbucks on every corner, Australians seem to prefer a cornucopia of one-off individual choices, each attempting to satisfy a coffee-crazy crew.

Think of a couple of parameters that your clients care about the most. Plot the position of your company on a grid like this to see where you lie relative to your competition. Some of the possible parameters include the line from the cheapest to the most expensive, the biggest range versus a select curated range, off the shelf to tailor made, in store to online.

Start by plotting where you are now and indicate where you want to move to if you'd be better off doing so. Sometimes a fresh consideration of just what your customers' two most important things are can lead to a significant innovation to satisfy what they want.

Brand permission

Brand extensions can be very successful. Rather than seeing their customers go elsewhere to satisfy their craving for an espresso coffee, McDonald's added McCafé to its restaurants. However, when they tried to launch a line of McDonald's hotels in Switzerland, people thought that stretched things too far and they closed.[18]

Where could you extend your product or service? Where would customers who know your brand think you'd gone beyond what they associate as a natural fit for it?

Return on effort

In the early days of your business, you tend to welcome any customers who will pay you. This is the 'any warm body will do' phase. After a while, you've usually collected a range of clients of varying types and sizes who pay differing amounts and require different levels of time and resources to fulfil.

When you reach the stage where you're getting what you consider at least a reasonable level of income but you're working around the clock, it's time to sort out who your ideal client really is. I've found it useful to do this using an assessment of ROE. You may be familiar with ROE standing for return on equity; in this case the letters stand for *return on effort*.

Plot a graph with a horizontal axis from hard to work with to easy to work with, and a vertical axis rising from low profit contribution to the highest. Place your clients on this graph. Your ideal clients are in the top-right quadrant. Treat them like gold. Clients in the top-left quadrant are making you good money but are hard work. We'll label them silver and try to figure out how to make working with them easier. Clients in the bottom-right quadrant are easy to work with but don't make you much money. We'll label them bronze. Try to increase their volume of work. Or put your prices up.

Clients in the bottom-left quadrant are tough to work with and not making you much money. We'll label them lead, like lead in your saddle bags. These clients are probably costing you and your team time and energy that would be better spent on others. Get rid of them.

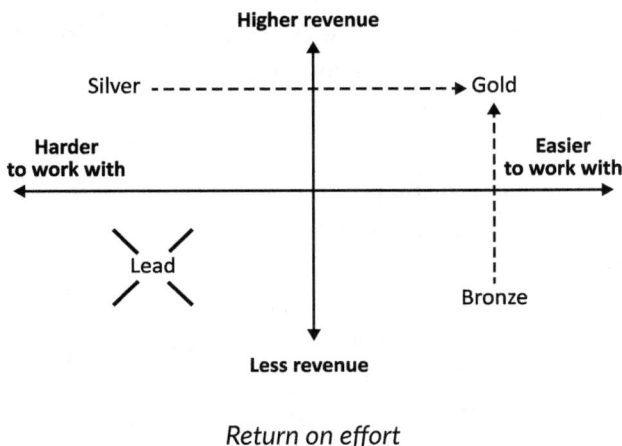

Return on effort

CASE STUDY: MERCHGIRLS

When I started working with the joint founders of Merchgirls, they'd got their business up and running and were starting to get established for providing better quality, sustainable promotional merchandise.

The problem emerging was having a large volume of differing types and sizes of clients, each requiring a lot of setup work to design their bespoke range of merch.

I worked with them to classify their clients, first of all by the dollar value of their jobs and then by the time and resources, and the effort it took to design, produce and deliver their merch. We ranked them from D through to A and AA, and added on AAA as an aspiration they hadn't got to yet.

When we examined the effort each class of client took, they realised the D class clients took almost as much effort as the As. The reason was the effort to design a budget range of merch for a low-volume order was not much different from the effort to design a range for a high-volume order.

As the girls wanted to do a great job for all clients, the fixed costs weren't much different. However, they were barely making any money on the D class clients, while the A+s were proving profitable. This allowed them to focus their outgoing marketing and sales efforts to connect with A+ potential clients and gradually decline the smaller orders.

Over time, they realised there was another classification they needed to pay attention to before discarding the Ds and Cs. They were clients who might dip their toe in the water with a small order as a trial, but who had potential to go on and become an AAA class client if satisfied.

Over three years, this strategy and the work we did to increase the effectiveness of their team and their operation in other areas, backed by their unrelenting work ethic and commitment to excellence, empowered them to increase their gross income by 600% while increasing their net profit by a similar margin, which they charmingly called 'that little figure at the bottom'.

It sounds obvious in hindsight, but until you discover your own financial accelerator, believe me it is not. For your businesses, your gas pedal may not be the volume size of your order. It might be the length of time they remain a client, the number of repeat orders or the type of product they order that can be knocked out quickly. It could be an order of level up from that, eg, the number of stores you have, where the stores are located or whether you own or lease. It could be whether you can deliver your service through using offshore talent, by automating some steps or by dealing with clients as a group instead of individually.

For service companies like lawyers, accountants and other groups that bill on a time basis, there's a formula that will fit most organisations:

Volume of jobs × billable hours % × $ per hour = gross profit

Now you can work on strategies that will improve each of those factors:

- Volume of jobs – better marketing and sales

- Billable hours % – productivity and efficiency improvements

- $ per hour – intrinsic brand value and positioning as authority

Whatever your economic driver is, try using the ROE model to help to work it out, as once you do, it will make a big difference to 'that little figure at the bottom'.

Summary

- Your value proposition is the summary of what your customers will value so much they'll be delighted to pay you to get it. Without a strong value proposition, your business won't get through the first stage gate and won't scale. Sadly, without this you will fail. So, if you don't have one, work on this first.

- Your brand positioning sets you within the context of your industry and how you compare, providing certain characteristics that a niche of customers want. Mapping the battlefield can help you decide where you should move to maximise your potential to grow and scale.

- Plotting where your customers fall on a graph of return on effort can help you focus on which customer types to cherish and which to say farewell to.

5

A Complete And Remarkable Solution

Have you ever been down to the beach, on what looks like a perfect summer's day for lazing around, taking a swim and spending some time in the sun, then retreated under an umbrella before you and your family get too fried? Then, after a while, a wind springs up and before you know it your umbrella gets picked up and flies down the beach, threatening to impale a small child?

On a holiday on the Queensland Sunshine Coast not many years ago, I arrived for a day on the beach, thinking about hiring an umbrella, when I saw several of what I learnt were called CoolCabanas. They provided a larger patch of shade from a square top sheet. Strips of cloth hanging down from each corner had ground-level pockets to fill with sand to securely anchor the CoolCabana in place. Simple but effective.

Architect Mark Fraser was on holiday in Noosa when he devised the concept with some sketches in the sand. In an article in *The Courier Mail*, he describes the process.

> 'I set myself the brief of wind and shade requirements, usability, and ease of carrying it and setting it up. [...] I made some prototypes and tested them, and every time, we'd have five or six people ask us where they could buy it.'[19]

He rapidly raised more than he asked for from a crowdfunding campaign in Kickstarter and got going. Demand has steadily increased ever since.

This is an example of a complete and remarkable solution. Complete because it leaves nothing out that you would want in this type of product. Remarkable because it's so good you tend to naturally tell other people about it.

I bought one for us and another two for my adult kids' families and flew them back to Melbourne. Now you see them everywhere and they have spread to America. Mark has gone on to create other innovative products like a shopping trolley made from recycled plastic.

Is your product or service a complete solution to your customers' needs? What might be missing that, if included, would make it so complete and amazing, people would call up their friends to tell them about it?

Jobs to be done

In 1990, Tony Ulwick created a process for innovation based on the theory that people buy products or services to get a job done, or rather a string of jobs done.[20] The traditional beach umbrella only got some of those jobs done, leaving the opening for a new product that got all the jobs done.

Unless you spend a fair chunk of time thinking about and listing all the components of the jobs that your product or service does and what other jobs customers want done, you can miss opportunities for innovation and capturing more customers. The jobs you think of first are probably the functional ones, but there are also emotional, financial and social jobs.

In considering whether your product or service provides a complete and remarkable solution, start by listing all the jobs your customer wants and needs to get done with the general type of service or product like yours. Take some time and start listing them on Post-it notes as they occur to you. You can order them later by their place in the customer journey. It's likely you'll start off with a handful, but keep thinking and you'll be surprised that there are lots of things your customer wants and needs.

Consider this list for selecting the services of a digital ad agency. Here are some of the jobs you might want them to do:

- Understand my business

- Appreciate the industry and trends

- List competitors

- Compare my products or services with competitors

- Understand my customers

- Develop insights into what drives customer buying decisions

- Analyse the best channel to approach potential customers

- Develop a new branding strategy

- Design a new logo and associated material

- Develop a new website

- Create material for the website

- Set up the search engine optimisation (SEO)

- Video some client testimonials for the website

- Write the headline and punch line

- Set up a way to capture interest and offer value to potential customers

- Make sure it's all viewable on mobile as well as on laptops and desktops

- Create a social media thought-leadership campaign

- Use educational PDFs as lead capture tools on the website

- Link it to an email database and autoresponder system

- Set up measurement of each stage of the marketing pipeline

- Monitor website visitor data and make improvements

- Create and run a Facebook paid ad campaign

- Create and run a Google ad campaign

- Set up campaigns for Instagram and other media

- Consider and advise on possible sponsorship of social media influencers

- Consider traditional media and advise on TV, radio, print, outdoor

- Develop a PR campaign and manage it

All of this is in the context of other jobs to be done such as:

- Providing a great service at a competitive price

- Responding rapidly to enquiries

- Being enjoyable to work with

And, of course, in the context of results:

- Bringing my brand to much greater awareness

- Bringing in lots of my ideal clients

- Generating a good return on money invested

The point of doing a list like this is to assess what gaps you might have in providing solutions to a comprehensive list of what customers want done.

Successful businesses tend to go one of two ways. They either provide an end-to-end service that takes care of everything or they concentrate on a narrow slice of highly specialised expertise, like search engine optimisation, and do only that for customers who want the pinnacle of cutting-edge capabilities in that field. Which approach should you follow?

The answer to this lies at the intersection of your passion, your capability, the market needs and the financial opportunity. Where can you stand out in a crowded world and find a tribe of customers that you serve better than anyone else?

First in class and best in class

In the world of medicine, research scientists in academia and biotech and pharmaceutical giants are all in the game of creating better ways of fighting disease through the discovery, development and introduction of new drugs, devices and diagnostics.

When a new breakthrough drug is launched that treats a disease in a new and better way, with a new approach or novel mechanism of action, it's known as first in class. These drugs, if they are safe and effective, as all the extensive requirements of the FDA and other regulators require, can generate significant new income streams for the company. However, as soon as other companies get a whiff of the potential of this new way of treating a disease, they'll be working on creating their own drug candidates that could be even better.

They must be conscious of any patents the company behind the first-in-class drug has filed, but with a clever team of scientists they may be able to invent a new candidate that doesn't infringe those patents. The race is on to create, test and launch what could become the best in class.

When I worked for GSK, a division known as Allen & Hanburys had recently launched a new drug for asthma called Ventolin.[21] This wasn't the first in class for bronchodilators, which provided rapid relief for asthmatics by relaxing the smooth muscle lining of

STARTUP, SCALEUP OR SCREWUP

the airways. Several other drugs had preceded it over half a dozen years beforehand. But it turned out to be the best in class. The chemists had managed to create a molecule with more specificity, which meant they had reached the top of the pyramid of what could be achieved in that class for several decades to come. Because of that it became a financial bonanza that underpinned the growth of GSK for fifty years.

Have you built a product or service that is so effective in producing the outcomes your customer wants that it's unlikely to be bettered, making it best in class?

Innovation

The original management guru Peter Drucker said the two fundamental functions of a business are innovation and marketing. The rest are there to support them.[22]

Often innovation begins when someone gets fed up with what exists now and believes a better solution can be found. Grant Petty went to a country town school in Victoria that happened to have a TV studio and a couple of computers he learnt to use. After leaving college, he went to work making TV commercials in a studio where he started to think about the immense cost in those days of the equipment and how that impeded what creative people who weren't working for large companies could afford to do.

Sometimes it's the intersection of two disciplines that opens an avenue for innovation. In 2001, Grant put his knowledge of both television and computing to use founding Blackmagic Design. He set out to change the Australian TV industry and ended up changing it worldwide. His first product was an innovative, inexpensive SDI capture card that improved the digital capture of video without the compression that computer products normally use. Grant went on the road for years showing the product to as many people as he could. He did trade shows, seminars and reseller events. Grant said he was never home. It was successful when people saw it and had it explained, but he had to get it out in front of people, so they understood the change it represented – how they could build their own television company.

That gave Grant the insight that products are not just a failure or success. There is a phase in-between where a new product is not successful yet; where it is received well by the customers who see it, but most people don't know about it. So, you have to build the product's awareness before they transition from 'not successful yet' to a success. Often the second or third versions are the ones that really click, as feedback from users and refinements lead to a product that ticks all the boxes.

Grant and his growing team went on to design industry-leading digital film and live production cameras. Over time he acquired several other companies, including Fairlight audio postproduction, and colour correction company DaVinci Resolve, to which he added editing capabilities, to fill out his vision of providing cutting-edge tools that reimagine what's possible, often at a more affordable price.

Since then, Grant's constant commitment to hiring smart creative engineers and empowering them to be as creatively free as they can be has led to Blackmagic Design becoming the standard many Hollywood movies turn to for video cameras, switching and postproduction. Now with over 3,000 employees and factories in three countries, he believes as Australians we need to rethink our attitude to manufacturing and intellectual property, to move beyond our stagnant reliance on government, mining and property for our economic future. He believes manufacturing something with impeccable quality and delivering it to people in volume is a marvellous way to take care of people and make a difference in their lives.

Grant's advice to the next generation of innovators coming through is to focus intensely and almost exclusively on making an exceptional product. Empathise with your customer and their problems, but then ruthlessly take the development of your product to the edge of what's possible, without caring what people think. Don't get tied up by investors or others distracting you with too much demand for data, regulation, or a need to build in layers of middle management. A great product, followed by another, is the main thing.[23]

Business model

Businesses exist and survive as structures
to solve problems people are willing
to pay to have solved.

You may be passionate about what you do, and you may have considerable expertise in an area, but if you don't have an effective business model, you aren't going to get far. Sometimes opportunities coalesce when new trends and technologies come together.

CASE STUDY: VINOMOFO

Vinomofo is an online wine buying business that curates a small selection of quality wine bought at significant discounts and provides delivery to customers on a 'love it or return it' basis. It's been a big success, but as co-founder Justin Dry explained to me, it was about his fourth attempt to put together a business around wine. Justin had come from a family with a strong history in wine and he was passionate about doing something in the space. There was an online travel show called *Road to Vino*, and another called *Qwoff*, which was based on friends chatting together and reviewing wine, and then one called the *Great South Australian Wine Adventure*, which had people downloading an app to win a trip or a year's supply of wine. Each had some appeal, but none had worked as a business.

As Justin explained to me, he and his partner hadn't understood what people were willing to pay for and had come at it from their own perspective, not the customer's perspective. While travelling in South America using Facebook for the first time to stay in touch with fellow travellers there, before it had arrived in Australia, and knowing Groupon was coming with online 'deals of the day', Justin started to put together another idea, despite the protests of his brother-in-law partner. They'd already built up relationships with producers and young wine buyers that allowed them to put the Rubik's cube of a successful business model together, drawing on the new trends in technology and social interests.

They knew they couldn't compete with the Dan Murphy's of the wine world by offering the biggest range, but they calculated they could actually beat them on price if they made a small collection of carefully selected wines and bought those in major volumes. They created an online community of younger wine lovers and offered them a limited and well-curated list of quality wines at significant discounts, with funky emails that spoke their language.

Vinomofo helped open up a younger audience through digital and social channels and helped a lot of interesting smaller wine makers tell their story to an audience that cared. They essentially said: you know we're wine lovers and you trust us, let us curate this selection of wines for you and we guarantee that they're going to be super-interesting, amazing wines. And if you don't like anything, send it back, full refund. On top of that, it's going to be the best price you'll see it anywhere.[24] The result was an 'overnight success', ten years in the making.

When considering whether you have a good business model, consider these different elements:

- Expertise

- Social trends

- Emerging tech

- Customer and industry connections

- Customer needs

Can you creatively bring them together to design a business model that gives you a competitive edge, profitability and scalability?

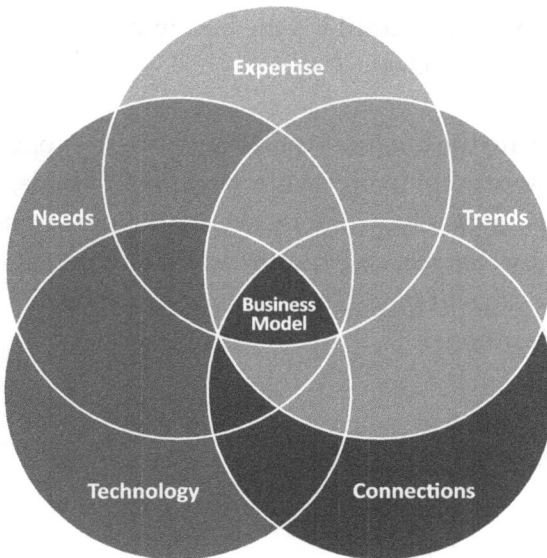

Elements of a business model

Summary

- A complete and remarkable solution that does all the jobs customers want done will prompt word-of-mouth recommendations that help spread awareness and interest.

- Creating a product or service that is a step function better than alternatives should be your main focus until you have more demand than you can easily handle. Without this, it will be difficult to scale.

- When you innovate and take a new product or service to market, don't stop innovating and improving it until it's the best in class, not just the first in class.

- Create the business model by bringing together your capability and your customers' needs, with new technology; taking account of new trends, your contacts and resources. Play with making the cogs fit together to generate a profitable operation.

SPRINGBOARD 2
PLANNING

Design from the future, then pull the present to it

'As many more individuals of each species are born than can possibly survive; and as, consequently there is a frequently occurring struggle for existence, it follows that any being, if it varies in any manner however slightly profitable to itself, under the complex and sometimes varying conditions of life, will have a better chance of surviving and thus be naturally selected. From the strong principle of inheritance, any selected variety will tend to propagate its new and modified form.'

This is how Charles Darwin in 1859, many years after careful consideration of his findings from the voyage of the Beagle around the Galapagos Islands, expressed his theory of evolution in his groundbreaking book, *The Origin of Species.*[25]

Darwin provided the evidence to prove species were not immutable, but rather evolved over generations to adapt to the environment they found themselves in. Through random changes in the genetic double helix of DNA, which took another hundred years to discover, the members who happened to be best fit for the purpose of survival would increase in number, while those not fit for the purpose would diminish and face extinction. Each business is also subject to the laws of natural selection within its world. Our jungle is an environment where changes in the economy, in society and in technology force businesses to adapt or die; where other businesses and other interests compete for customers, for employees, for finance. Business owners must accelerate the evolution of their products, their services and how they run their businesses to survive and fulfil their purpose.

6
Purpose, Mission, Vision

Fit for purpose

Is your business fit for purpose?

'Fit for what purpose?' you may ask.

Exactly. Have you specified for what purpose you're running and building your business?

Let's start with a personal purpose. Most business owners will have a vague idea in their minds that the reason for – the purpose of – starting their own business is to make more money, provide better for their family, get more time for themselves and enjoy life more than working for other people. How's that going?

If your business is falling a little short on some of those goals, it's probably because you haven't yet got a business that is designed to fulfil that purpose. What would a business look like that can achieve those goals?

Before we can design it, list the things you want your business to achieve in detail, with completion times. For example, you might want it to be:

- Profitable enough to pay off your mortgage in three years' time

- Productive enough to be home by 5pm every day to play with your kids

- Running well enough without you to take a month's holiday without loss of momentum

- A positive disrupter in your industry to provide superior benefits to customers

You may have several more objectives, but let's start there. Now we can think about what must happen to achieve them.

Profit

Let's start with profit. A lot of would-be entrepreneurs will start with a goal in mind of making a pile of money.

If you had asked smart businesspeople a couple of decades ago what was the purpose of business, they'd have quoted economist Milton Friedman who said, 'The sole purpose of a business is to generate profits for its shareholders.'[26]

Should they have received a classical education, they might have quoted Adam Smith from his seminal book, *The Wealth of Nations*, published in 1776. Here Smith describes 'the invisible hand' that provides unintended social benefits from an individual's self-interested actions.[27]

But as Quaker Oats President Kenneth Mason said, 'Making a profit is no more the purpose of a corporation than getting enough to eat is the purpose of life.'[28] Making a profit is necessary, of course. Naturally you want to make substantial growing profits, and that should be a goal. But that comes not from the direct *pursuit* of it, but *as a result* of fulfilling a useful social purpose. One that customers value sufficiently to pay to have satisfied. One that employees care about sufficiently to feel their work is meaningful and worthwhile. One that should be the unwavering guiding light for your organisation.

It seems authentically pursuing a social purpose beyond shareholder returns is actually beneficial for financial returns.

Research by Deloitte has shown that the top issues consumers identify with when making decisions about brands are: '28% how the company treats its own employees, 20% how the company treats the environment and 19% how the company supports the communities in which it operates.'[29]

Purpose-driven companies experience higher market share gains and grow three times faster on average than their competitors, all while achieving higher workforce and customer satisfaction.

Intrepid Travel was founded to deliver responsible travel. It uses local accommodation and transport, recommends nearby cafes and uses local guides. In this way it gives tourists a more authentic experience, while ensuring money is spent in the places they travel to in a way that benefits the local communities. It open-sourced its own animal welfare policy and toolkit for other tour companies to use. While it was badly hit by Covid lockdowns, it's now bouncing back to its former strong growth rates, with the ambition of being the world's first purpose-led, billion-dollar travel company.[30]

Your business purpose

Every business should have a purpose and a mission. People get confused between the two terms, so perhaps a short story will help.

Have you ever seen the 1980 movie, *The Blues Brothers*? [31] This cult classic, starring John Belushi and Dan Aykroyd as two criminal brothers who decide to do some good, used to play regularly at the Valhalla Cinema in Melbourne, with packed audience participation that was as entertaining as the film. People would come dressed in the same dark suits and sunglasses, sing the songs, call out the key lines and even throw pieces of toast in the air when a toaster in the film spat its contents a couple of feet in the air.[32] It was great fun.

The plot follows Jake Blues when he gets out of jail. He and his brother Elwood visit the orphanage they grew up in and hear that the place will have to close if it can't raise $5,000 by the end of the month. Following an epiphany at a blues gospel church, they decide to go on a 'mission from God' to save the orphanage, getting their band back together to raise the money.

What follows is a wild, crazy race around Chicago, attempting to put on concerts to raise the money. Meanwhile, they're at times confronted by the girlfriend Jake left jilted at the altar, who attempts to kill them with a flamethrower and a rocket launcher. They're also encouraged by classic blues legends like Aretha Franklin and chased by at least 100 police cars splintering through shopping malls, causing absolute mayhem. Yet eventually, somehow, they raise the money and save the orphanage.

If you ever get the chance to watch it (and you should), you'll get the point. The Blues Brothers were not going to be stopped, because they were on a 'mission from God'. Mission and purpose are intertwined.

Their purpose was to save the orphanage; their mission was what they did to achieve it, getting the band back together and raising the $5,000.

What inspired you and still inspires you as your mission and/or purpose with your business? Maybe it's like some of these ambitious ones: [33]

- **Google:** To organise the world's information and make it universally accessible and useful.

- **Tesla:** To accelerate the world's transition to sustainable energy.

- **Disney:** To make people happy.

- **CSL:** To save lives around the world and deliver sustainable value for our stakeholders.

What's your mission in a nutshell, if you forget false modesty and bravely step way out there?

Michelangelo said, 'The greatest danger for most of us lies not in setting our aim too high and falling short, but in setting our aim too low and achieving our mark.'

> Dreaming large has its benefits, even for us mere mortals. It forces us to think differently and play a bigger game. You're more likely to come up with innovative ways to grow by considering how to be ten times bigger, rather than just a little bit bigger.

Maybe your mission is as simple as serving the best flat white coffee in town. No easy task, mind you, if you're in Melbourne. Whatever your mission is, make sure it's based on making a difference to a group of people you care about. As Sir Richard Branson said, 'a business is just an idea to make people's lives better.'[34]

Vision

Most businesses strain to press forward a little from where they are each quarter, trying to increase sales, keeping a lid on expenses and striving to make marginal improvements to what they're doing now. It's like shovelling more coal into the furnace of a steam train to eke out a little more speed as it chugs up a mountain track and that's hard yakka.

A better way to plan your growth is to take a helicopter ride to the top. Travel out three to five years from now and see what your business could look like – no, what it *will* look like – when it's achieving its mission and satisfying everything you want from a business. Take an hour sometime, when you're uninterrupted, to daydream on paper just how you'd like things to be.

Vision statement

How big and what shape would your organisation need to be to achieve your dreams? Where would you be operating and how? Who are your customers?

What services or products would you be providing them? What level are your sales and profits?

What would your organisational chart look like? What role are you playing in the organisation? How much time are you spending on the job? What is your culture like? What impact are you making in the world?

Make your vision statement as detailed as you can, describing it as if you were telling someone what it's like living in that future time, operating the way you want to. Leap ahead past your current stage to at least the next stage – or even two stages ahead – to imagine your business at that level. Check the list of things from the table in Part 1 that you'll need to be focusing on at that stage.

What does it feel like to have your business like that? If this feels anything less than great, then adjust your images of how things are until it does feel great.

A day in the life of you

When you've got your vision statement written – if you wish, including some sketches, drawings or other visualisations done to your satisfaction – spend some time imagining what it's like living a day in your life at that time. Write this up in the present tense, describing things that are happening now that you're there.

Where are you living now, in what house, with whom? How does the day start for you? What's your routine before work? When do you work, what do you do on a regular day? Who are you working with? What are you concentrating on, to forward the action at that stage for your business? What are you enjoying the most? What are your employees saying about working in your organisation? What are your customers saying? What do you do later in the day and at home?

Allow your imagination to envision how you'd like things to be without limitation.

Work backwards

Now that you've spelt out your vision for the business at that time, look back to a step before that. Say, a year before it. Let's call that Intermediate Stage 2. What would the shape and characteristics of the business need to be at that stage before moving on to the finished vision?

From that, look back and see what the organisation would look like a year before that. Call that Intermediate Stage 1.

Now, having done that in reverse, you have two stages spelt out from where you are now to where you want to be. This exercise will make it easier to see what your next steps are. It'll help you plan things, like who to hire next, when to move to bigger premises, if and when to raise money, and so on.

Don't worry that your vision statement or the intermediate steps are not fixed in stone. Think of the three-to-five-year description as a rolling vision that will inevitably change as you progress and unforeseen events crop up. Revisit it and the intermediate steps once a year to update and review it for use in your annual budget and personnel planning.

It's easier to see how to climb a mountain when you're looking back down from the top. There's an inspiring, if perhaps apocryphal story that when Michelangelo was asked by the Pope how he created his famous marble statue of David, he answered, 'I created a vision of David in my mind and simply carved away everything that was not David.'

Summary

- Define the purpose you started your business for to satisfy your own needs and wants.

- Define the social purpose of the business and the mission it must go on, in terms that can inspire you and your team to stretch and grow as people, as well as a business.

- Detail, as your vision, just what your business will look like in three to five years, at the next stage or beyond, imagining it has achieved or is well on the way to achieving your personal and social purpose.

- Look back from there, rather than forward a few months from where you are now, to create a plan with the steps to get there.

7
Strategy

Now you've defined your why and what, it's time to work out how. Strategy is one of the most misunderstood parts of business planning. It's not really planning. That should come afterwards.

> Strategic priorities are not strategies,
> they are objectives. Strategy is how
> you reach those objectives.

Virtually all companies set so-called strategic priorities or have strategic plans each year. These tend to be a series of objectives that are 'strategically important' rather than just tactical. They often include statements like these:

- Increase our sales by 20%

- Decrease production costs

- Improve employee engagement
- Double our conversion from marketing

They mostly miss the mark in extracting the possibility of what a creative strategy can achieve. They tend to be all planning, no potential.

Real strategy can do a lot more than inch forward; it can redesign whole industries. Before Tesla, the prospects for electric cars and where they might be positioned in the crowded car market were a puzzle. In 1997, Harvard University professor Clayton Christensen published a book called *The Innovator's Dilemma*, about the history of how innovation had disrupted a variety of industries.[35] In the book he describes how innovations like smaller disk drives for computers initially entered sectors at the bottom of the market. They were typically ignored or dismissed by the dominant players for their inferior technology and inability to satisfy their major customers.

The dilemma was that it made sense at first to ignore them. But over time these new entrants gradually stole market share by offering benefits such as affordability, smaller size and convenience, despite initially inferior quality. After a while these new entrants improved quality and performance to the point that those larger customers took them up. Some years later they became dominant as the previous leaders were locked physically and mentally into continuing to do what had previously worked so well.

Innovation doesn't always arise in this manner. Professor Christensen had a chapter devoted to electric cars, in which he struggled to find a role for them but speculated that their future might lie in their use as cheap, safe vehicles for learners, as they were so slow. Even though he was a pre-eminent researcher in the area of innovation, he didn't anticipate the benefits of new battery technology or how Tesla would approach the introduction of their electric cars.

If Elon Musk had followed the path Christensen described, he would have initially launched a cheaper but inferior car, then gradually improved it over a few years. However, Elon knew that the public opinion of electric cars was an obstacle to any widespread adoption, so he came up with a different strategy.

His first car was a sports car, but the real breakthrough came with the launch of the Tesla sedan, which offered the startling benefits of the space and luxury of a top-end sedan with the acceleration of a Ferrari. That combination was so unusual that for years, YouTube featured surprised supercar drivers being outdragged by a Tesla.

In combination with this revolution, the Tesla was also the first car to reposition the automobile as a piece of mobile software. This made it capable of improving rather than depreciating after purchase, with online software updates. Tesla's other revolutionary goal was to produce a truly self-driving car. The perfection of that is proving a lot more difficult than originally anticipated on public roads, where there are so many potential situations the software may not have been programmed to deal with, but automated trucks are running successfully in controlled situations like mining operations.

The car, the production line, the technology, even the way the cars are sold; everything at Tesla was designed from the ground up, rather than as an incremental improvement on what came before. With the combination of different strategies and new technology, Tesla is on the path to fulfilling its declared purpose of accelerating the transition of transport to sustainable energy.

In considering strategy for your business, think about where your capabilities can change the game, in alignment with achieving your mission. Where can you play and how can you win? It may be as simple as focusing solely on a narrow target market to supply a growing demand for deeper expertise in the area.

CASE STUDY: TALENT NATION

Talent Nation was started by Richard Evans in 2012 as a recruitment agency. Nothing new there, except that Richard decided to focus solely on sourcing people to fill positions for environment, social and governance (ESG) roles (as he always believed that business could be used as a vehicle for delivering positive social and environmental outcomes).

Richard was making a name as the expert in the field and Talent Nation became a founding B Corp in Australia; a certification that requires measuring your company's entire social and environmental impact. The business grew relatively slowly until around 2019, when companies and the investment community turned their focus to ESG and demand for talent in this area accelerated.

Around that time, Richard became a client of mine and we started to implement the springboards described in this book to equip the company for sustainable growth. We worked through how he and his partner wanted the company to operate in three years' time, building the culture and performance needed from their developing team. They put the right processes in place to measure progress, while not losing sight of the ethos of the company. A key change was for Richard to stop being the problem solver for everything within the group and to make the shift from operational work to leadership work, while still being the voice and face of the business.

Over the next two years, revenue grew by over 400%, staff numbers doubled and Talent Nation became the recognised leader in the niche.

Creating a strategy for growth

If you don't already have a strategy for growth, consider your potential in each of these categories:

- Shift how you compete in current markets

- New market segments

- New product or service innovations

- Partnerships (even with competitors)

- Mergers and acquisitions

Initially, brainstorm possibilities of what you could do with your capabilities, passions and resources, without criticism. If we don't turn off our analytical minds for the first stage of this process, we'll be too quick to kill off initially wild sounding ideas that could turn into useful prospects.

Once you've done that and got several in each area, start to sort them – putting them onto Post-it notes, if you like – into several categories. Plot them or place them on a graph like this one, plotting ease of implementation against potential medium-term profit.

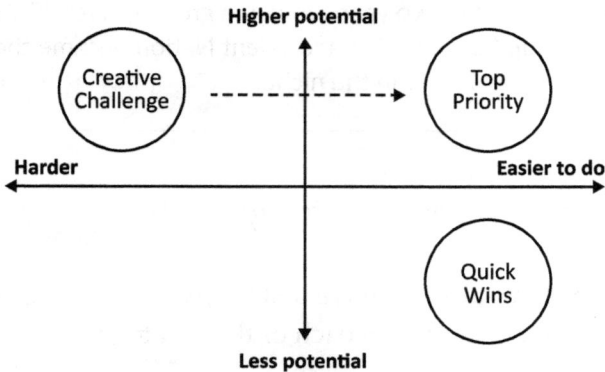

Growth strategy choices

Carving out a niche

Strategy can have a major impact on your ability to carve out a niche in competitive markets.

Most airlines in the US operate on a hub and spoke model, whereby you fly into a major city like Chicago or Denver and then onto your final destination. This has some benefits for the airline, but for the customer it can mean issues collecting and re-presenting your bags, and delays at the hub with a change of aircraft.

Southwest airlines started in Texas and decided to fly direct between cities like Dallas and Houston. It also strove to be a low-cost airline, using only one type of aircraft while providing more benefits than other airlines, like included luggage and flight change flexibility. Perhaps their biggest advantage and the reason they have grown across the US to hold nearly 20% of a competitive market is that their approach and service makes passengers feel the airline is run for them, and not just the owners.[36]

Richard Branson's Virgin Atlantic service sought to differentiate itself from competitors like British Airways by appealing to passengers wanting more fun and entertainment in the spirit of other Virgin businesses. He tells the story of how when he wanted to spend $10m to install video players in seat backs, the banks wouldn't lend him the money. So, in a rather large lateral leap, he asked Boeing if they would supply a new order of planes with video pre-installed. When they said yes, he got the banks to lend him $1 billion to do it.[37]

CASE STUDY: QANTAS

I had my own experience, developing a strategy to differentiate Qantas flights. After leaving my audiovisual partnership, I was offered a job in one of the advertising agencies we had done some work for. I ended up turning down the offer from McCann Erikson but did accept a consulting job to come up with a campaign for their client Qantas to distinguish its domestic flights (known under the banner of TAA in those days) from their rival of the day, Ansett. Before putting pen to paper, I asked if they would set it up for me to fly around the country to experience what both airlines had to offer.

In those days, aircraft had a small first-class section of a few seats up front and then it was economy for the rest of the plane. Off I went for several days, flying up and down the east coast on both airlines in their economy sections. Security was relaxed in those days and after chatting to the pilot on one flight, he invited me to sit in the cockpit while he landed the plane in Hobart, which was fun.

There was nothing that I could see to tell the two airlines apart and I spent a couple of days trying to think of smart advertising plans, but it wasn't too long before another more striking thought took hold.

It became obvious that there were two distinctly different groups of people flying in economy class.

There were businesspeople, who wanted to arrive on time with some energy left over to get the day's work done and, if possible, return home in time for dinner. They wanted a quiet experience, to be left to doze or prepare for the work that lay ahead. Then there were people mostly going on holidays or flying to visit friends and family. They were in a jubilant mood, looking forward to fun times. They wanted a different experience, more like 'let's get this party started!'

I realised that while the *apparent task* had been to create an advertising campaign for an existing service, the *real* or *deeper task* was to differentiate the offering in order to satisfy what the customers in each segment needed and wanted.

I wrote a report recommending that Qantas (TAA) separate their economy class into two new classes. Business class would be up the front, where business travellers would board by the front stairs, and be mostly left in peace with a paper and cup of tea. Holiday class would occupy the rear section of the plane (perhaps with a sliding curtain to adjust for how many of each class were booked). They would board by the rear stairs and be treated as though their holiday was starting there and then with some fun, games, entertainment and a few drinks.

After a few months, via conversations between the agency and Qantas (to which I wasn't invited), they decided to go with a form of business class and ignore holiday class. That was the world's first business class air travel. Business class has subsequently turned out to be popular and profitable with most airlines, but I still think the concept of holiday class was a missed opportunity.

The other missed opportunity was mine. I was paid what I thought was a reasonable fee at the time for a young chap, but with the benefit of hindsight I should have asked for free lifetime business class travel.

Summary

- Strategic priorities are really objectives that need a strategy to achieve them.

- The biggest gains can come from figuring out your strategy more than your objectives.

- Use strategy to solve and overcome any obstacles in the way of reaching your objectives.

8

Financial Tracking And Governance

If you're an accountant or have had financial training, this section may seem a little basic. If you haven't come from that sort of background, getting up to speed with financial reports can be somewhat daunting. It may be one area where you're happy to leave it to the experts.

> As fish swim in the medium of water, a business lives and moves through numbers and while you don't need to become an Olympic swimmer, you should at least learn how not to drown.

While you're still learning about financial analysis you'll be relying on your accountant, so it's useful to understand their usual approach.

There's a somewhat unkind joke about accountants that goes like this: 'How do you tell the difference between an introverted and an extraverted accountant? Well, when you're having a conversation with an introverted accountant, they'll look down at their shoes, whereas the extraverted accountant will look down at *your* shoes.'

Jokes aside, many accountants can fairly be accused of driving while looking in the rear-view mirror, meaning they spend most of their time constructing and reporting on what happened to your business last year, as their primary role historically has been to do the tax for your previous year. It can take some searching to find a more proactive accountant, or some prodding of your present one to get them looking forward and providing financial advice to help improve how your business performs in the coming years.

Even without specific training, you're probably already being supplied with and getting some familiarity with reading a profit and loss (P&L) report and an end of year balance sheet. These are necessary but are not the only, or even the best, templates for guiding the future growth of your business.

Cash flow forecasts

Data from accounting software company Xero shows that UK, Australian and New Zealand small businesses operate in the red – ie, they're cash flow negative – for about one-third of the year.[38]

The single most useful financial template to under-stand and track is a cash flow budget. While it's useful to also do a P&L budget, cash flow is more important, since – strange as it seems – you can go broke running out of cash while making a profit.

P&L accounts operate on an accrual basis, meaning when an invoice is sent after you've made a sale, it's entered into the P&L accounts and goes towards assessing if you've made a profit, despite the cash not having landed in your bank account. It may get there in thirty days, or it could take much longer if your debtors delay payment. Meanwhile, you need to pay your bills promptly. That delay in getting the cash into your account, if repeated and stretched out for longer, could cause you to run out of cash to make those payments. That's how you can become insolvent, despite your P&L showing you're on track to make a profit.

Directors of a company are legally required to cease operations when the company can no longer pay its bills as and when they fall due. When the cash runs out, it's game over, and that would be a level ten screwup.

It's easy to set up a twelve-month cash flow budget on a spreadsheet or in software like Xero, or else ask your accountant to do it. I've illustrated the simplest version for three months in the following figure, but I recommend you do it for your full financial year and fill out more detail within your income and expenses.

Note that it's cash receipts reaching the bank over the course of that month that we're counting as income and cash payments leaving the bank that month that we're counting as expenses.

Each month should have three columns: one for the forecast budget figures, one for what actually happens and one for the percentage variance. Now every month it's easy to track cash in the bank to see if you're winning or losing and make decisions based on real and timely information. You can see the effect of, for example, a downward trend in sales, or delays in getting paid, or rising expenses in particular areas. When businesses do go broke, they usually haven't had this basic up-to-date information and only realise how deep they are in doo-doo too late to make the necessary corrections.

When you have a budget forecast like this, you can also use it proactively to test different scenarios. You can model different possibilities for the business, such as asking what happens if you employ two more salespeople. Drop their expected expenses into the spreadsheet and then adjust the sales up enough to restore the profit to what it was before. Now, the difference between the previous sales and this forecast is the breakeven minimum extra sales you need to justify hiring the sales guys or gals. Like stepping on the scales to check your weight, this makes decision making tangible and it becomes easier to see whether you should make the investment.

	Month One			Month Two			Month Three		
	Budget	Actual	Variance	Budget	Actual	Variance	Budget	Actual	Variance
Opening cash at bank									
Income 1									
Income 2									
Income 3									
Total cash receipts									
Expense 1									
Expense 2									
Expense 3									
Total cash payments									
Net change									
Close of month cash at bank									

You can model other things like what you think the effect would be of developing a new product or service line, or putting your prices up. You can run scenarios based on a change in the business environment, eg, a pessimistic scenario to cover a situation with, say, a pandemic or recession, by estimating a reduction in sales to see what you would have to cut in expenses to stay solvent.

Reverse income statement for forecasting new product income

There's a further simple trick you might find useful. We're switching over now from cash flow to a P&L model. Let's say you're contemplating developing a new product or service and it's hard to accurately forecast sales; that even expenses aren't easily forecast, but you need to know if it's going to be profitable. The answer lies in tipping things on their head.

Instead of starting with sales, start with profit – but not the forecast profit. Start with the *required* profit: the profit you need to have to make the process worthwhile. Put that in first.

Think about what level of sales you'd need to have to get that much profit. Your spreadsheet will tell you what level of expenses you'd have to limit the process to in order to get the profit required.

Using this method changes it from a forecast without much evidence to a creative challenge. Now put your team to work creating ways to reach the sales needed and inventing ways to make it within the budget.

Don't stress too much if the expenses look way too high initially. This may provoke a total rethink of how to do things to get under the allowed costs; rather like when Space X had to design rockets that for the first time could land and be used again to make space flights affordable.

Desert island dashboard

When you're driving down the road in your car, it just takes a glance to check your speed, the fuel level and whether there are any warning lights. In many modern cars you can also check how many kilometres or miles you have to go before you run out of fuel, when the next service is due, the tyre pressure, the oil temperature, the revs per minute, whether you're over the speed limit, if you are moving outside a lane or too close to the car in front, the outside temperature, whether the handbrake was left on, and so on. Shouldn't you have a similar dashboard that gives you immediate access to key information about your business?

Imagine yourself on an extended holiday. Your business is nicely set up and running well without you, but once a day – or, even better, once a week – you want to check how things are going, just to reassure yourself before going back to the swim-up bar. What data would you need to glance at on your phone or laptop?

Different businesses and people will want slightly different figures, but here is a list to start with:

- Sales vs targets

- Enquiries

- Leads

- Conversion rates

- Client satisfaction measures like NPS (net promoter score)

- Expenses vs budget

- Debtors total and timeline

- Quick ratio (liquid assets as a ratio of liquid liabilities to check capacity to pay bills)

- Cash at bank

Other measures may include:

- Safety

- Employee efficiency

- Major objectives progress metric

A longer-term measure to keep an eye on is return on equity (ROE), more specifically net profit after tax as a percentage of total equity. The significance of this measure is that it tells you what profit you've made with the funds that shareholders (whether that's you or others) have invested. You can compare this with what other potential investments like property or publicly listed shares might return, to see if you're doing better or worse than using the capital elsewhere. An ROE of 20% is generally considered a good objective for successful small businesses.

Get your accountant to set up a dashboard for you with these or other measures you want; or find a software plug-in (known as click and drill), such as Syft or Castaway; or else use Microsoft BI to pull the essential highlights from your data. You may just decide you can move to Bali, or at least relax for a longer vacation, while occasionally – and only occasionally – briefly checking on your business before turning back to the beach.

Valuing your business

What's the end game for your business? Do you want to sell it, pass it on to the next generation, let employees buy in, be granted some shares, or bring in a partner? How do you or others decide what your business is worth? Ultimately, beauty is in the eye of the beholder, but there are some guidelines.

The value of well-established businesses can be calculated by assessing the discounted value of all future profits. To do this, you forecast what you consider will be the profit each year, taken out for a period of, say, twenty years, discount them by a risk percentage relevant to the particular industry and then again by a percentage representing the weighted average cost of capital, ie, the appropriate interest rate, since a dollar today is worth more to you than a dollar next year and that is worth more than the following year, and so on. This calculation gives you a net present value. However, for early-stage businesses forecasting all future earnings out for twenty years is wishful thinking. At the 1998 annual Berkshire Hathaway meeting, Warren Buffett described intrinsic value as, 'the present value of the stream of cash that any asset generates from here to doomsday. That's easy to say and impossible to figure'.[39]

Often a rule of thumb multiple is applied to earnings (profit) before interest and tax, or earnings before interest (EBIT), tax, depreciation and amortisation (EBITDA). To get a valuation for the business, this figure will be multiplied by somewhere between one and five, according to the industry, the length of time the company has been operating, the predictability of earnings and the growth prospects.

A refinement of this method is known as the capitalisation of future earnings, where a weighted average of the past three years pre-tax earnings is adjusted, if necessary, to account for their likely maintainability and net tangible assets are added to come up with a valuation. If you have any intellectual property, or a strong enough brand to add some value for any intangible asset, so much the better.

In practice, valuing a company is not just an objective calculation. An investor or industry partner will be influenced by the mood of the day about the economic outlook, the risk or promise of particular technologies or industries, their confidence in management and other factors.

CASE STUDY: HSBC

I spent several years building an investment management company – with my co-founder Peter Attwood, who was an early pioneer in technical analysis – adding to my more fundamental methods and looking after the share market holdings of high-net-worth individuals.

We went on to sell the company to the global bank HSBC and worked for them as fund managers, looking after hundreds of millions of industry superannuation fund investments and advising on billions of investments in resource companies.

The prevailing wisdom of the day was that the price, ie, the price quoted for a company listed on the stock exchange, rationally reflected its real value every moment of every day. It seemed obvious to me that wasn't true, since prices could fluctuate quite markedly over a few days with no change of information on the company or the economy, and they were obviously wildly overvalued in boom times and wildly undervalued near the depths of a recession, for example.

The clincher for me was the 22% drop in value of the US stock market in one day in October 1987. What had changed was nothing substantial in facts, but the rapidly shifting mood of investors from optimistic to fearful, with an ensuing mass attempt to exit all at once, resembling a stampede of cattle reacting to gunfire.

After joining HSBC and thinking about how to better avoid being caught on the wrong side of this kind of calamity, I worked with a team of econometricians to develop a mathematical model of the stock market that plotted the fair value of the market and various sectors, based on inputting relevant factors that influence business conditions and profitability. There were many factors, like productivity, wages, inflation, exchange rates and commodity prices that had an influence, but interest rates and sentiment turned out to be the biggest.

The valuation of your business will also be affected by the mood of the times, the enthusiasm for and assessment of risk in particular industries and by interest rates. Regardless of the ups and downs in external factors, you can make your business as appealing as possible by having the accounts in good shape. This will not only help you to sell your business when the time comes, but it will provide a useful discipline to help you understand the reality of how your business is travelling, to proactively fix early problems and seize opportunities for growth.

Governance

As your company matures and as you set it up for potential sale or new investment, you need to put more formal governance arrangements in place. The ad hoc meetings and hurried considerations of progress and decisions need to be replaced with a regular structured process of review to improve performance and reduce risk.

Initially, this is likely to be done with an advisory committee or board who meet once a quarter. Some key items for an agenda for these meetings should include:

1. Attendance and apologies

2. Acceptance or revision of previous meeting's minutes

3. Matters arising from previous meeting

4. Reports on key metrics of the business over the last quarter

5. Highlighting of any major deviations from forecasts

6. Consideration of any significant external changes affecting the business

7. Any strategic matters for discussion

8. Decisions on significant financial expenditure plans

9. Actions arising from this meeting

10. Call for any other matters

11. Date of next meeting

Such an orderly and regular review is a good discipline to check progress, assess risks, review opportunities and make well-considered decisions from a perspective a little removed from the rush to complete daily activities. Right process = right result.

With an advisory or formal board, look for a chair who – while they may have had considerable experience in larger companies – has worked with smaller ones as well. This is important because the context of decision making is different with a small company. For example, as a large well-established company planning to raise capital, you would be willing to wait to do at this at the most advantageous time for maximising the price you can charge investors for your shares. However, as a small company you often can't afford to wait as the window can slam shut on you in a way it won't with larger companies.

When the biotech company for which I was the CEO was planning to list on the Australian Stock Exchange, we had everything lined up – or so we thought. We had a licence deal with Merck – one of America's largest and most prestigious pharmaceutical companies. We also had the support of Macquarie – one of Australia's largest stockbroking companies – to conduct the listing.

However, a week before we were due to list, the terrorist planes flew into the Twin Towers in Downtown Manhattan and our plans fell with them. Overnight, no one wanted to invest in a small risky biotech and we were politely told it was game over, so far as listing in the next year was concerned.

> Large companies should raise money strategically. Small companies need to do it opportunistically, anytime they can.

Summary

- Cash flow forecasts vs actual spreadsheets are the first and arguably most important financial tracking tool for small businesses.

- Create a list of a few key measures you want to watch and organise them on a dashboard to check regularly whether or not you're on a desert island.

- Set your business up for sale, even if you don't plan to sell it, as it will help you keep things shipshape and spot problems early on.

- Establish an advisory board and later a formal board with a chair who understands businesses of your size.

SPRINGBOARD 3
PEOPLE

Build a team that takes total ownership

Take a moment while you're reading this to rub two fingertips together. Pause for a minute and give it a go. Can you feel the fine ridges that make up your fingerprint? How would you describe that feeling?

Would you be surprised to know that in fact there is no feeling in your fingertips? When you experience the sensation we call 'feeling', it's because disturbance of some proprioceptors has set off electrical impulses that travel up the sensory nerves to the somatosensory cortex, where the sensation is constructed and interpreted within a region mapped out in size to reflect the numbers and importance of the nerves.[40]

Cut those nerves and you no longer feel anything in your fingertips. Yet, a direct electrode stimulation of that part of the brain will trigger a feeling as if something had touched your fingertips.

We live in a world of experience simulated in our brains. We assume what we see, and experience is reality. Except we don't *assume* it's true, we're *certain* it's true, as we never realise it's a series of assumptions.

That confidence, for the most part, serves us well. Our mechanisms of perception are designed to provide shortcuts to avoid having to freshly interpret literally millions of inputs a day. We rapidly learn to become pattern recognition machines that instantly react. We couldn't have survived without them as a species, hunting for food without becoming something else's lunch.

Unfortunately, those automatic shorthand judgements can make life more difficult as we react to other people in today's social and business world.

9
Team

A matter of perspective

Have you ever noticed how different people talking about the same incident at a dinner party, or an important office meeting, can have different memories and accounts of what happened, who did what and how people reacted?

We're biologically programmed to bypass making fresh assessments. We jump to opinions based on our prior history of experience with people that seem similar and subconsciously remind us of an emotional reaction to some previous experience. We tend not to hold these opinions lightly: we identify with them and will fight to prove we're right.

Our individual differences make being part of a functional team much more difficult. Yet, if you're going to accomplish a difficult mission, you need an effective team to get it done. Getting past the $1m and particularly the $4m stage gate is not going to happen without the right team performing the right way.

You can't do it on your own and you can't make other people do things. The days of authoritarian leadership are over. You're going to need a team that wants to be there and will do what's required because they want to.

We've all had experiences of good teams where it's a joy for people to come to work. Things just get done, people back each other up, you get the results, and you go home feeling energised and content. We've all had experiences at the other end of the spectrum too. Sometimes absence makes things clearer than when they're present.

A few years ago, I invested a small amount of money in a start-up biotech company before it was listed. Almost a year later, I went along to the first annual general meeting of the company. The managers, scientists and investors were all there, listening to various resolutions being proposed.

After a while, I noticed something strange. The scientists were voting one way and the managers the other way, every time, in opposition to each other. I put my hand up and asked what was going on. They stopped the meeting and explained that there'd been a break-down in communication and trust.

It turned out the managers believed they'd told the scientists they were going to get their shares after the company listed on the stock exchange. The scientists, on the other hand, believed that they were going to get their shares immediately. They couldn't agree on the issue and relations had become embittered.

Instead of discussing the content of their original agreement, or any new arrangement, it became personal. The scientists said the managers knew nothing about the technology and without them it was going nowhere. The managers said the scientists were over-inflating their self-importance and the technology was never going to get commercialised and make a profit without them. Any progress with the development of the company products had ground to a halt in a level eight screwup.

> Where you have a lack of common understanding, relationship and respect, people often retreat to protect their self-interests, and all trust evaporates.

As I hadn't been involved, I perhaps somewhat fool-ishly offered to assist. It took six months with lawyers at phone-point, but eventually we decided to take all the existing agreements, put them in the bin and start again. We gave the scientists their shares upfront and gave one of the scientists a seat on the board of directors, so they had total transparency over all major decisions in the company. Gradually, trust began to redevelop.

Having been through that experience and several other attempts to build teams – with some occasional success – and seeing the ups and downs of other teams I'd been a part of, I've come to the conclusion you need the following five things for 'team' to be present. Team as in a sense of, yes, there's a functional team present here.

Five elements of team

1. Empathy

The foundation is empathy. Often when we get busy, we treat relationships at work as transactional: I pay you, so get that done and get it done by 5pm Friday.

People don't respond so well to that anymore. Authoritarianism is kind of over, at least in the modern Western business world. People know they're there to get work done and that's why they're employed, but they also want a relationship for its own sake. They want to feel valued, to believe that you actually care about them. They want you to listen to what's on their minds, to understand their needs. They want transparent communication, straight talking and fair dealing. They want you to walk the talk, not to say one thing and do another.

We might still hope that people will show up at work, park their external stresses at the door and operate as uncrackable productivity superstars. Occasionally you might get such a person, but as the leader of your business, you'll need to spend some time understanding their internal world and being there for them as more than an old-school boss.

Your reaction, like mine, may be to think, 'Hold on, how much time is this going to take?' It takes as long as it takes for them to feel heard and in a relationship. Mostly that can be accomplished with a few informal words or a quick roundup of what's happening at the start of a Monday morning meeting.

I chair a peer advisory group of small to medium business leaders, under the auspices of a CEO networking group called The Executive Connection (TEC). At the start of every meeting, we have a brief 'sign-in', where members comment for a couple of minutes about significant events in their lives and in business. This process never fails to connect the group and establishes a sense of mutual relationship. On that foundation, work can rapidly proceed.

2. A common mission

It's somehow more obvious in younger people, but people have always responded positively to a common mission. They want to know what they're doing is worthy of their time. That there's something inspiring about it, something that is worth their blood, sweat and tears, if that's what it takes. They want to believe in the organisation's purpose, in its vision. They want to share the passion, and you want them to share the passion so that people show up at work energised and delighted to be there.

They'll also want to feel that the values of the company are kind of aligned with their personal values. If there's a significant misalignment of values, after a while either the individual will opt out or the culture will spit them out. That's why understanding people's values is so important when you're hiring.

Of course, people also want to know they can advance their careers and be paid a competitive rate. You should have considered bonus schemes and whether they are better done as team bonuses, rather than individual ones. Employee share ownership plans (ESOP) can be appropriate as you grow and seek to retain high-performing people. However, money is usually not the only – or even the major – driving factor. They want to feel heard and appreciated, they want to have some autonomy about how they achieve their objectives, but most importantly they want to believe in a common cause and see progress towards achieving it.

3. A culture of respectful challenge

The third thing I feel you need is a culture of respect. As we said before, part of this is shared values, but there's more to it than that. Obviously, there's integrity, like a feeling that each person is valuable. Every person *is* valuable.

Now that doesn't mean that you can't have disagreements. In fact, as World War II General George Patton is said to have put it, 'If everyone is thinking alike, then somebody isn't thinking.'

Ray Dalio, who founded Bridgewater, which became the world's largest fund manager, established a culture of radical transparency and respectful disagreement.[41] He wanted to create an idea meritocracy. People were encouraged to challenge, confront and question each other to get to better outcomes, but to do so in a respectful manner: from a ground of respect and helpfulness, rather than point scoring by making the other person feel wrong. So, respectful challenge.

4. Diversity

Everybody has their strengths and gaps. When I went to school if you were doing poorly in, say, maths, they made you do more maths. What they should have said is, 'Forget maths, you're good at literature, do more of that.'

We now understand that everyone has their inherent strengths and gaps, and you can't change that much. You want people to work in their areas of natural strength and have other people fill in their gaps if they have natural talent in that area. In that way, you create a team with a spread of broad and deep capability.

Value the strength that every individual has and understand there's a diversity of opinion, skills, knowledge and perspectives based on experience and training. If we draw on that diversity, we'll all be better for it.

5. Accountability

The fifth element is accountability. If you want results, people have got to be accountable for what they say they're going to do. You want to be listening for the language of accountability. We live inside language, and we relate to others and work with them using language, but we're generally not as aware as we could be of the power and the nuances of that language. Can you hear whether someone is going to get something done or not? Ask for commitments and follow people up on keeping them. This is how you get outperformance.

Fixing what may be missing in your team in those five areas is a leadership challenge of both utmost importance and difficulty. It starts with recognition and acknowledgement of the current reality. Improvement will require you to facilitate conversations for the team members to accept the challenge and honestly engage in a mission to build a better team.

If you've got those five factors present – empathy, a common mission, a culture of respectful challenge, diversity and accountability – 'team' will be present. With the aligned, committed action of that kind of team, you can break through any barrier.

Summary

- See if you can catch your own automatic reactions getting triggered by situations and people in time to pause and reflect before speaking or acting, and notice other people's triggers.

- Consider if you have a functional team operating in your workplace and rate it out of ten.

- Look for what is missing from the five key elements listed in this chapter, if you're not satisfied.

- Lead the team in self-recognition of the issues, the need to change and co-creating a plan to improve.

10
Communication

Speech acts

As business leaders, our job is all about communication. Do people understand and buy into what we say? Will they engage and commit to taking on necessary tasks that we ask them to take on? Can we hear how people are going, not just in their jobs but in their lives?

Our ability to communicate is fundamental to our success in our roles. To get where you are now, no doubt you already have good skills in this area, but can they be better?

There are several different types of communication for different tasks.

Communication for understanding

When someone says something to me, if I'm being honest, I often catch myself thinking about whether I agree with them or not or beginning to think about what I will say when they stop. I'm in my own head, listening to my own thoughts, instead of listening to them. This is particularly the case if the conversation is a little heated, or in some way triggers some feelings on either side. Here, a tool known as active listening is useful.

After the person has said something, you respond, 'Just so I can be clear I've heard you correctly, let me repeat what I believe you're saying and tell me if I'm wrong.'

This has several benefits. Firstly, knowing that you're going to have to do that snaps you into paying focused attention to what they have to say in the first place. Secondly, they can correct any misheard elements to clear things up and get a common understanding. Thirdly, if they've delivered the first round with some unbalanced heat, it gives them a chance to reflect and adjust that, having heard their own words fed back to them.

Communication for innovation

New ideas are like newborn babies. They don't survive unprotected in the jungle. The savage beasts in the jungle of business are our own critical minds.

If we operate in the usual manner, the instant a new idea is proposed, we'll form an opinion on what we think of it and we'll usually find it hard to stop ourselves speaking up to shoot it down.

Without some structure, a meeting to ask for or discuss new ideas, or proposals for innovation, can too rapidly be closed down.

First, ask people to refrain from any criticism of a new idea, no matter what their unstoppable internal thoughts are. Instead, ask them to add any far-out extensions or projections of their own. Often an absurd first thought can lead via an equally absurd other thought on to a practical idea, but first, we must defang the lethal nature of our own opinions. We hold onto our opinions as if they were a part of us, and as if criticism of our opinions is tantamount to criticism of us as people. It would be better to spread opinions, unattached to any person, on a table to be looked at with a curious mind and compared unemotionally with other points of view.

As a second phase we can begin to consider how we could make one or more of those ideas into something that could be tested.

A third and final stage allows more critical assessment of the feasibility and viability of the best of the ideas, before choosing which to take forward.

Communication for relationships

Until you're in a state of relationship with whoever you're talking to, there's little prospect of getting them to understand or act on what you have to say.

In casual conversation, we do this all the time by commenting on the weather, some sporting event or news of current interest. We're warming up and getting in sync before talking about other things.

In a business setting, this can work to a limited extent, but it helps to think about what's already on the mind of your audience and addressing that before wading into the meat of your intended conversation.

I once had the job of writing a speech that the head of GM's truck division was giving to a large gathering of GM truck dealers. I'd done my research with some dealers and discovered they were pretty pissed off with some aspects of the way they believed they'd been treated.

The gathering was intended to announce some new trucks, but I realised that unless the head of GM acknowledged their concerns at the start, they'd be thinking about their issues rather than listening to what he had to say about the new range. So, I wrote an opening that freely admitted the issues and the intention to fix them before outlining the rest of the announcements. It did the job and helped heal the relationships at the time.

Communication for action

Have you ever been frustrated, asking someone if they'll do something only to get the reply, 'I'll try' or 'I'd like to'? I think we all suspect when we hear that kind of language that it won't get done.

There is a set of words that make it much more likely things will get done. They're called speech acts.[42]

> Most speech is a description of something else, like a thing or a feeling. But a promise is an action. When someone says, 'I promise', they're making the act of a promise. When someone says, 'I request that you do this', they're in the act of requesting.

There are other words that are also speech acts, which tend to be associated with having more power and consequence. Speech acts like declarations and commitments.

Use speech acts in business conversations where you need certainty that action will follow. If you want to have a powerful meeting, require that people only speak in terms of promises and requests. Instead of saying, 'Well, I'll try to do that sometime next week,' have them think about it a bit more deeply and make a promise they can commit to. If they need assistance to deliver on their promise, have them make requests and not just wishes. When you make clear requests and promises, you'll find the productivity of your meetings, of your individuals and of the whole team, rises strongly.

In fact, if you want to double your productivity, double the number of requests and promises you make.

Listen for the subtext

We instinctively know when someone's being genuine, or when their words say one thing and they mean another.

At the dysfunctional end of the spectrum, you have someone who insists on procedure, or doing it 'their way', when what they're doing is deliberately making things difficult. They might feel unappreciated, they might have a bone to pick, or they might have a gatekeeper mentality that is seriously making teamwork less productive and more stressful than it needs to be.

At the other end, however, are people who seem to be complaining, but are expressing a problem that actually needs fixing, or insisting on a standard that must be met, or making a request of some kind in disguise.

Listen for the underlying, unspoken message to decide if the problem is a situation that needs fixing or a person needing counselling and reflection – and failing improvement, departure. Listen for whether people are committed or not.

When you deliver on your promises and don't make idle requests, when you make a request clearly and listen for whether the other person can commit or needs backup, this builds trust. Trust is another vital element in making things happen with a functional team.

Summary

- When you want to be understood or want to understand another person, particularly under pressure, use active listening to focus, get clear on the matter and destress.

- If you want to give new ideas a chance to fly, don't shoot them down before they've left the nest.

- Before people can hear you, they need to feel they've been heard and some connection is present between you.

- Listen for and use speech acts like promises, requests, commitments and declarations for powerful communication that's far more likely to get results.

11
Recruit, Engage, Retain

Get the right people onboard

One of the tougher challenges most leaders have is finding and recruiting the right members for the team. You've probably had the experience of setting out to find a great person for a role, and after sifting through a shortlist you pick someone who shows up for an interview and seems impressive. You check out their references: they seem to get on with people, they can tell you how well they performed and what they've achieved in the past, so you hire them. After a while, to your horror, you find out they can't actually do the job. What's going on here?

Well, you probably didn't look closely enough at their behaviour, habits and values to see whether they matched your culture and what you need in the job. For example, if you are hiring a salesperson, what are the habits that you need? Well, one thing you need is discipline. You want your salesperson to call a certain number of people a day, whether they feel like it or not. So, when you're interviewing them, you might ask them, 'Tell me how discipline shows up in your life, or how you've used discipline in various areas of your life.' It helps to hunt down your own references that they haven't offered and ask if they're a disciplined type of person.

You also want to know that they can cope with being told 'no'. That's another area where you might want to enquire how they can demonstrate that they can deal with being told 'no' and persevere. There's a story about a sales manager who told every sales candidate the same thing at the end of their interview, 'I'm sorry, but you just don't measure up to the standard we're looking for.' This was said to everyone, no matter how well their interview went. Most people, on hearing this, mumbled something like, 'Oh, I'm sorry, I hope I didn't waste too much of your time,' as they sidled out the door. A few said something like, 'What are you talking about? I've just explained to you how I can markedly increase your sales. You'd be mad not to hire me, since I am exactly the person you need.' Those are the salespeople who got hired.

There's a small caveat here, as salespeople tend to fall into two camps. They are either hunters – like the ones who got hired in the story – or farmers, who while they would have failed that test may be good account managers for repeat customers, as they are a gentler breed, more focused on nurturing relationships. You must decide if you want a hunter or a farmer and understand their actual behaviour and whether that's going to suit the job that you need.

You can, of course, use a recruiting firm to help you find and assess a shortlist, or you can use a psychometric tool to sort through candidates after they've completed a test.

There are many personality and skills assessment tools, but one of the best I've come across is the Predictive Index.[43] It's intended to help you hire with certainty, lead with purpose, build cohesive teams and keep your people engaged. Their software assesses people's behavioural drivers to assess whether they are naturally suited to a particular type of work. You can define what you need for a role, or else draw on their list of roles and their compiled experience of the personality types and behaviours that would best fit. The software will rank candidates in order of suitability so if you get a lot of applications, you can just interview the top few.

Another way of assessing a candidate is to have your whole team spend some time with them, perhaps in a more relaxed setting like a Friday afternoon drink. If you have managed to develop a great culture in your company, they won't let anyone who isn't going to be a good fit get in.

It also makes sense to take on new people on a trial basis of, say, six months, by which time you should know whether you want to make their position permanent.

Employer branding

All of that is about how to assess people who apply for a role in your company. But what if you're struggling to find enough reasonable people to even run through some kind of test? What if you just aren't getting applications?

Employer branding is important if you want to become the employer of choice. How do you present the benefits of working with you to attract the people you want?

The first thing I observe is that most job ads are so deadly dull it's no wonder companies struggle to attract candidates. The worst of them are written in dubious jargon; the best are, at best, clear about the job, the responsibilities and the qualifications they're looking for. But where is the personality of the firm? Where is some sense that this is a human-centred organisation that, while it takes its work seriously, doesn't take itself too seriously? Where is the language of real people having a chat together about spending the majority of their waking hours in each other's company?

> Take a risk and show some personality in your job ads, in the kind of language you might use over the phone to a friend who you wanted to work with you. Then you might attract enough quality candidates to form a decent shortlist.

According to a 2022 Gallup survey of workers around the world, only 21% were engaged in their daily work as an average, while in Australia the figure was an alarming 17%. The most common complaint from disengaged workers was that they had little respect for their boss and considered they were treated unfairly. Business units with engaged workers have 23% higher profit compared with business units with miserable workers. Additionally, teams with thriving workers see significantly lower absenteeism, turnover and accidents; they also see higher customer loyalty.[44]

One aspect we all must consider now is whether to offer remote or hybrid working arrangements. Some research says while basic productivity can be maintained or even increased with the flexibility of working from home, camaraderie and creativity suffer without fairly frequent and extended face-to-face time.[45]

Total time at work is another factor. There are some companies, like Australian consulting company

Inventium, who have gone to a four-day week and who report an increase in productivity as well as a reduction in stress.[46]

Finding the right mix for your business starts with examining how best to achieve all your outcomes, including financial and human factors. In the modern world, you're likely to get a better result by including your team in discussions about the options and what would work best, rather than handing down a dictum.

There's an ongoing shift in these areas towards a more inclusive environment. People want more autonomy with expectations of being part of decisions around working conditions, and they enquire into the values and social purpose of the organisation they work in. This doesn't look like a trend that will reverse.

Values and culture

In the long run, the culture of your organisation will arguably have more effect on your success or failure than anything else.

> Culture is how your employees behave when no one is watching. Their individual and collective values drive decision making. Culture drives behaviour, and the end results are the actions taken that determine the success – or lack of it – for your company.

A lot of companies have now posted their corporate values in their tea rooms, their boardrooms and on their websites. We're all familiar with the chasm that often exists between those values and the typical behaviours that prevail.

In the early days of building a new business, the company values will consciously or unconsciously reflect the founder's personal values. As you take on more than a handful of employees, it soon becomes clear they don't all automatically have the same set of priorities in their list. At this stage, you realise you need to articulate your company values and find a way to encourage all employees to operate by them.

How do you avoid having this operation produce a list of 'blah blah' values that get posted on a wall and promptly forgotten? Where do you get the list of values from anyway?

One effective way to go about it is to run a workshop with your team, so they feel they've been heard and had some input. A good place to start is not with your own personal values but with what your customers value in doing business with you.

What do customers say when they've had a great experience buying and using your product or service? Do they say they loved your responsive service, your expertise, how the product made them feel, the value for money or the way you looked after their interests?

Following on from that, what do your employees say they value in working for and being part of the company? Do they love being empowered to be creative, make a difference and be part of a champion team?

Of course, there are also going to be values that, as founder or CEO, you insist are intrinsic to the culture you want to develop within the business. Perhaps it's being customer-centric, going the extra mile and fostering innovation.

This is best tackled as a two-part process. Firstly, have the discussions and then develop a list of no more than five key values in plain vanilla English. Secondly, have a go at turning those listed values into the hot chocolate version, with more memorable short funky phrases in the vernacular of your organisation. If they're written in a way that reflects the spirit and personality of your company, they are far more likely to be remembered, and more importantly, to become living guidance rails for expected behaviour.

Australian-founded software company Atlassian has done this for their values, which they say guide what they do, what they create and who they hire. The first of their values is: 'Open company, no bullshit.'

It can also be useful to write up a sentence or two following each value to give more context into how that value is expected to be expressed and followed. The way Atlassian expands on their first value is:

'Openness is root level for us […] we understand that speaking your mind requires equal parts brains (what to say), thoughtfulness (when to say it), and caring (how it's said).'[47]

One rotten apple

Have you ever noticed how one apple in a bowl can affect the others? Once an apple is rotten or gets significantly bruised, it produces ethylene, which increases its internal temperature, leading to a breakdown of chlorophyll and, at the same time, the synthesis of other pigments. The starch in the apple gets converted to simple sugars and simultaneously a component of fibre called pectin that cements the cell walls together begins to disintegrate, which softens the tissue. More ethylene is released affecting nearby apples, which starts a chain reaction.[48]

Until you've been through it once or twice, it's easy to make some mistakes with managing your team. One of the classics is finding out that one of your staff isn't a team player. Quite often this individual is a high performer, perhaps the rainmaker for the company, either the top salesperson or the leading tech head. However, when they're in discussions with other members, they're quick to point out when they think someone else is wrong. They do it in a personal way, criticising not just the ideas or opinions but the intelligence or worthiness of the other person. When you attempt to pull them aside to have a chat about this, their answer is likely to be, 'But I'm not wrong, am I?'

They're also quite likely to hold on to key information and even data that should be shared or recorded for the whole company, considering it's 'their IP'. They want to be indispensable, but you should dispense with them.

Despite your fear of losing whatever they produce, you need to appreciate the degradation of other team members' morale and motivation that they cause. They're toxic to the culture you're trying to create and their effect on other team members will gradually lead to disenchantment and other people resigning. In other words, a high-level screwup. When you finally summon the courage to fire them, you'll find other team members step up and do better, and their overall team output – as well as the mood – improves.

Right people, right roles

A different kind of mistake is putting round pegs in square holes. Often this happens because somehow, over time, you've collected a group of people and now you move them around to fill the roles and jobs that need to be done. What you haven't done – or at least not done well enough – is to first define the functions that need to be managed and then the skills, behaviours and personality types that would perform best in these roles.

If you do this from a blank sheet of paper and then objectively rate whether the current people in your key areas match the ideal characteristics of who you'd employ if they weren't already there, you may be in for a shock. If they don't rate an eight with prospects of becoming a nine, you have two avenues. Develop a training programme to get them to at least an eight, move them to a role they do happen to really be suited for, or say goodbye while helping them to move on. OK, that was three roads. But as Americans say, 'you do the math'.

There are people who say you should never fire anyone as it's not their fault, it's management's fault. I've found that if someone isn't suited for a role, you'll both be happier when they've found a role they are suited for, even if it's outside your company.

Assessing whether someone is well suited for a role can now be done with more than instinct. There are tools to help you work out people's natural abilities and personal drivers to assess if they're likely to shine in a particular role or not.

Patrick Lencioni, the author of an excellent book, *The Five Dysfunctions of a Team,* has developed a questionnaire he calls the six types of working genius. As the name suggests, the quiz helps you recognise the areas of your natural talents and the areas you may not naturally be suited for. His thesis is that it helps to realise what your talents are so you work in those areas and don't waste time in areas you're never going to excel in. His other insight is that it's advantageous to see that you have at least someone in your organisation that is naturally talented in each of the six areas, which he labels: wonder, invention, discernment, galvanising, enablement and tenacity.[49]

The better psychometric tests, like the Predictive Index, can also provide insights into the roles someone really should be in, how best to manage them to get the best from them and how they're likely to behave in a team.

Team stages

There are three stages that teams tend to go through.

Groundwork

In the first stage you're working on all the basics. What's the purpose of the whole mission? What are the resources that you need – the people, plan, roles and procedures – all those things that you need to have in place to start your mission?

In these circumstances, typically you'll put in ten units of effort and only get back one unit of return. Then, after what can seem like – and can be – a long time, if you persevere and have something of value, you kick on into the next stage. Generally, the last thing that you need in order to move on is accountability: people keeping their promises.

Momentum

When promises are kept and you have all those other factors in place, then you kick on into stage 2. In momentum, you're putting in the same ten units of effort, but now you're getting back ten units of results. This phase doesn't seem to drift but happens in a short period, like a quantum shift. Now matters are progressing with less resistance and things are suddenly beginning to flow. It feels quite different.

Customers are buying the products, the project is getting built. Productivity, delivery – it's all beginning to happen. Under these circumstances, strangely enough, you must communicate *more* rather than less, but you can communicate in a less restrictive manner perhaps.

Takeoff

To kick on into the next stage, what you need to have in place is team backup. What I mean here is that every member of the team, as well as doing their own job, is keeping an eye on other members of the team. If they see another member of the team struggling, they'll hop in there, back them up and help them get the job finished.

If you watch a good cricket team playing, when a fielder flings the cricket ball at the stumps to run the batter out, quite often it's not to the wicketkeeper but to the bowler's end of the stumps. In the heat of the

STARTUP, SCALEUP OR SCREWUP

moment the bowler might miss catching that throw, since they don't have the wicketkeeper's gloves or they're out of position. Now the team needs someone else who's anticipating that behind him or her, to sweep in and stop the ball. When your team is routinely backing each other up, you can then move into stage 3.

In takeoff, problems get fixed automatically and rapidly, opportunities are followed up and there's a great spirit of camaraderie. Now sales are growing and, at last, profits are seriously increasing too.

Level 3 teams

There can be a stage beyond this, where you can reinvent the game, if you have a level 3 team.

- Level 1 is where all your key individuals are highly proficient in their roles.

- Level 2 is where individuals also back each other up and act to defeat selfishness and silos from deteriorating team performance.

- Level 3 is where individuals take ownership of the whole organisation and its success. They automatically care about and take action for the benefit of the whole enterprise. They may or may not own any actual shares in the capital of the company, but they've taken ownership of seeing the organisation improve. They're on the lookout for how to achieve the bigger picture mission and vision. If you notice people doing this, hang on to them, reward and develop them. They are your next level of leaders.

I learnt the importance of this the hard way in my first business, producing audiovisual shows. We had grown rapidly and were taking on new staff. In the early days I was looking after conceiving and writing the shows, while my partner looked after production. As we got busier, my partner hired a new person to be the production manager, shortly before we took on a major new product launch that involved both film and a multiscreen slide show to introduce a new line of agricultural equipment, including combine harvesters. Both of us left the completion of this show to this new person and realised only too late that he was struggling to complete it on time and hadn't told us this was a developing risk.

On the night, with several hundred dealers assembled to see the show, the film only made it in time because we hired a private plane late in the afternoon to fly it down from Sydney, where the postproduction was being done. The slide show just wasn't finished in time to play it at all. The hollow pit in my stomach, as I faced up to telling the company manager we didn't have it ready, was not something I ever wanted to repeat. It was a level ten screwup that led to me deciding to leave the business.

What I learnt was to never again take less than total ownership for all aspects of a business. That didn't mean at all that I was going to do everything, but I was going to make sure that everything did get done.

Summary

- Use every means you can and take your time to find and hire key people. Nothing is more important to your success.

- The values your people live by guide the decisions they make. The company culture will shepherd their behaviour, for better or worse. Develop and nurture these guardrails to the actions they'll take, as they'll determine your company's future.

- Don't put up with a toxic high performer. If they won't change, say goodbye and you'll be pleasantly surprised at how the rest of the team steps up.

- Assess what level your team is playing at and let them know where you expect them to play and what that looks like. Take total ownership for the business outcomes yourself, and if you want to get through several stage gates and keep scaling beyond $4m a year, find key employees who will also take on total ownership of the mission.

12
Leadership

If you want to move past the business stage gates and bust through your growth ceilings, it could be said that you have one job: to be a leader.

But what does that mean? Leadership is one of those things we probably all recognise when we see it, or more commonly when it's needed, yet absent. It's rather hard to define or figure out how to build it in ourselves and others.

If we turn to the Oxford Dictionary, it says to be a leader is to lead other people in an activity or a project in an organisation. So, a leader leads (which is rather circular and unhelpful).

If you look at the literature of what leadership was considered to be, going back 100 years or so, leaders were thought to be just a few individuals with some mysterious qualities of being a leader. This was the 'great man' model of leadership. They were often talked of as being great communicators, with some kind of natural charisma and the ability to inspire people and make tough decisions.

Then people started asking, 'Could we train leaders? What are the innate skills and abilities that they have? Can we reproduce these in other people?'

Theories of different kinds of leadership popped up in an ever-accelerating list. There were situational leaders, transformative leaders, authentic leaders, servant leaders and stage 5 leaders, who were individually humble but doggedly committed to their cause.

As interesting as these all are, do they give you a path to being a better leader yourself? Can you change yourself to be transformative, or humble, or to take on any other prescribed characteristic? Does that really make you a leader?

The question I ask myself is not what leaders are *like*, but what do they *do*? What do leaders do that *anyone* could do, if they wanted or needed to be a leader at work, or elsewhere?

My working definition of what leaders do is this:

Leaders see a change that's needed and engage people to make it happen. Things that wouldn't otherwise happen.

I know a few people who seem to be born natural leaders. I was not one of them; it seemed risky to me. Probably because I had unconsciously learnt at a young age at boarding school that standing out was an invitation to get picked on. I was happy to let others take the lead while I did a specific job that interested me, but gradually I realised if I wanted to make things happen, there was no choice but to be a leader.

When I retired from the biotech company, I knew Australia had a lot of great fundamental medical research. But, with a few standout exceptions like the bionic ear, built on the research and dedication of Professor Graeme Clark, we had a poor record in translating and commercialising it.

I suspected the reasons for this were in part cultural, since academics were promoted largely on their publication record, and in part a lack of appropriate training. In the early stages of their career, scientists focus their research narrowly to become world experts and push the boundaries of knowledge to publish in that area. As they progress and succeed, if they make discoveries with commercial potential, they need to acquire a whole new range of skills. These include filing patent claims, assessing the financial value of their discoveries, finding new funding sources and pitching for them. They will need to secure industry partners and understand their data needs; negotiate contracts; prepare for the regulatory pathway, including clinical trials; understand the marketplace for new drugs, devices and diagnostics; and lead large multi-disciplinary teams. Yet, they had no training at all for any of these tasks.

I decided to have a crack at doing something about this. Together with a couple of like-minded people, I put together some basic training, cheekily called 'MBA in a Day', which gave them an introduction to business thinking. This garnered enough interest to get requests for a longer programme.

CASE STUDY: MOLECULES TO MEDICINE

In 2012, together with the Walter and Eliza Hall Institute and the Cancer Therapeutics CRC, I approached the Victorian government and secured funding to run a programme for three years, which I called Molecules to Medicine (M2M). This was a pilot to test the hypothesis that training could make a difference in the translation and commercialisation of research.

I thought such a programme would be welcomed with open arms by all the research institutes, yet while many individuals championed it and participated in the governing committee, other heads of research saw it as an unwanted distraction from pure research and publication. They resisted letting their young scientists participate. It was uncomfortable and frustrating at times, but there was enough support to get it underway.

M2M consisted of twelve months of training in all the facets of medicine development, with a particular focus on engaging with industry, since academic research often stalls in what's known as the 'valley of death' before clinical trials, unless some collaboration with industry can be achieved. Over the twelve months, the interns came together for a series of twenty expert seminars, workshops and team exercises and returned to their home institutions for on-the-job training and mentoring from their business development managers. Over forty expert speakers kindly gave their time to contribute to the programme.

At the end of the three years, 109 interns from sixteen different medical research institutions and universities graduated with a certificate of completion from M2M, co-signed by their own institutes.

Tangible results attributed to M2M included: nearly $10m in new funds raised from non-traditional sources, forty-nine collaborations with industry and twenty-five licences signed to commercialise their research. In addition, three new companies were spun out with significant input from graduates. Many graduates went on in following years to take up positions in industry or business development roles in research institutions.

Essentially, we had shown that entrepreneurship could be taught to scientists with no prior experience. I'm still in touch with several of the graduates, who are kind enough to say it made an ongoing difference to their careers.

It'll take a generation to shift the culture at the top of research houses, but M2M helped to move the needle, generating interest and awareness that much more was possible to make practical use of our outstanding science.

Looking back on this experience and on some classical examples of much greater leadership, I've done my best to distil some steps that anyone who wants to make a change can take.

The tasks of a leader

1. Assess

Leaders notice what others often don't. They see what's happening and call it out.

Winston Churchill spoke up about the gathering strength and dangers of Nazi Germany at a time when most European and British leaders just didn't see it.[50] When you are immersed in a situation that develops slowly, or has always been there, it's hard to imagine something else, or even notice what's odd about it.

When you first walk into a room, you can smell if there are fresh flowers or if someone's been smoking, but after a few minutes you don't notice it. Your sensory receptors have become saturated and the distinction between the presence and absence of the smell no longer exists.

Have you ever been to a foreign country and seen things that stood out to you as unusual that the locals were so used to they were hardly aware of? Take a fresh look at your business, your industry, with the eyes of a foreigner. What is really going on? What is the state of the nation?

2. Need

Leaders declare what's missing and describe how things could be better.

President John F. Kennedy borrowed a line from George Bernard Shaw when he said, 'Some men see things as they are and ask why. I dream things that never were and say, why not?'[51] Bill Gates realised that the mainstream pharmaceutical industry wasn't tackling third-world diseases like malaria and directed the Bill & Melinda Gates Foundation towards filling that gap.[52]

Look objectively at your business, as if running it through an audit. What's needed that's missing now? How could your business look if it was the way you really wanted it to be?

3. Stand

Leaders take a stand and won't be shifted from it.

President Zelensky of Ukraine, when offered an airlift escape by the Americans at the start of the Russian invasion in February 2022, said, 'I don't need a lift, I need ammunition!'[53]

What is going on in your organisation that you can take a stand on and refuse to tolerate anything else? What unmovable principles does your company stand for?

4. Mission

Leaders declare a mission and sketch a vision of a better future.

Martin Luther King declared, 'I have a dream that my four little children will one day live in a nation where they will not be judged by the colour of their skin, but by the content of their character.'[54]

What vision of how your company can operate in the future will inspire a mission to get there?

5. Enrol

Leaders enrol and align a team to take on a mission to achieve a common vision.

Who do you need on your team? What will inspire them to wholeheartedly engage and commit? What values and operating principles must be embedded?

6. Game plan

Leaders, together with key team members, develop a strategy to achieve their mission.

The founder of Ikea and his team developed flatpack furniture to make Scandinavian design cheap enough to appeal to a mass of younger home builders willing to spend their time assembling the furniture. What approach could you take to overcome obstacles, like perceptions or cost, to capture a significant share of your market?

What project management approach are you going to take? Does your mission require a series of short sprints with adaptation as you go, or does it need a more traditional critical path, longer-term Gantt chart type of management, to track, allocate responsibilities and update progress?

7. Resources

Leaders get the resources they need to get the job done.

What resources do you need to break through in your market? What left-field ways could you use to get them?

8. Adjust and persevere

Leaders make adjustments on the fly to get back on course and keep going to complete their mission.

Under Reed Hastings, Netflix shifted from mail order DVDs to streaming TV to making its own TV programmes, all in the name of providing great entertainment in a convenient form.[55]

Do you need to adjust, pivot or reinvent your products, services or manner of execution to stay on your mission?

Summary

- Leaders step up when they see a change they believe has to happen.

- It's not their personality or style so much as what they do that determines if they can succeed in creating the outcome they seek.

- There's a process that anyone who is committed to making something happen can follow to enrol people and take on a mission.

SPRINGBOARD 4
PROCESS

Make it repeatable, reliable, relatable

Bees are remarkable for their feats of organisation and process. Every bee has a distinct job and performs it with focused fervour. There are three types of honeybees: the queen, the drones and the worker bees. There's only one queen bee who produces all the offspring. Male drones leave the hive every day looking for other queen bees they can mate with, to extend the clan. Female worker bees start off looking after the queen and the larvae. They produce wax from the glands in their abdomens to build the honeycomb structure. As they age, they transition to flying out to collect nectar, pollen and water.

Nectar is sucked out of flowers and stored in their abdomens. Pollen is collected by over a million hairs on the bees' bodies, legs and even eyes, and passed back from leg to leg to a storage sac called a corbicula, where they can carry a third of their weight on their flight home. As they flit from flower to flower, they unwittingly but importantly pass on pollen from the male anthers to other plants' female stigma to promote fertilisation. Back at the hive, the nectar is stored for the bee's energy and the pollen is made into a form of bee bread that the larvae eat as they develop.

It's a sophisticated system that even includes the bees doing little dances, in which the speed of their side-to-side movements indicates the distance to a desirable group of flowers and the direction of their waddle shows them where to fly.

If you've ever looked inside a beehive, you'll have noticed it's made up of a repeating sequence of hexagons. Why hexagons and not some other shape? It turns out that hexagons are the most efficient form to maximise the use of any space.[56] Physicist Brian Cox points out it took thousands of years for mathematicians to prove this, but the bees have known it all along.[57]

There have been millions of years of evolution to get to this highly organised system that ensures not only the survival of the bees but also the survival of the ecosystem of many plants, without which we would also struggle to survive.

The way a company is set up to operate efficiently and in turn benefit customers, employees, shareholders and the community has evolved over a much shorter time span. Perhaps we haven't reached the sublime perfection of the bee colony, but we have the benefit of being able to consciously design and adjust our systems and structure as we go.

13
Systems Thinking

Zoom in, zoom out

Your business is a series of systems that operate within other systems.

A business itself is a system for providing something people value in exchange for a token of value we call money, which can be exchanged for other things of value. Businesses operate within a marketplace, within a system of domestic and international trade, in a system we call the economy, within a system of laws that operates within a system of government.

Within any business there need to be systems for developing products and services; obtaining customers; producing products and delivering services; receiving payment and paying bills; hiring, managing and motivating employees; health and safety; managing environmental impact; communicating with stakeholders; making decisions; and governing the enterprise.

Within each of these systems, there's a process that can be defined, measured and refined. These are like fractal patterns that continue down as you go more and more into the details of any part of your business, and out and out as you expand to consider how we all operate within the same world.

To a fair extent, along with culture, the effectiveness of these processes and their integration with other processes determines your success.

Comparing systems

When a fifty-two-year-old man who had been struggling to sell an occasional milkshake maker got an order for eight machines at once from a hamburger joint in San Bernadino, California, he was sufficiently intrigued to drive out to take a look. What he found was a couple of brothers who had turned the usual way of making and serving burgers into a more efficient system.

They had a self-service counter that eliminated the need for waiters. Food was delivered quickly, because hamburgers were cooked ahead of time, wrapped and kept warm under heat lamps. With these innovations they could afford to sell their burgers for half the price of competitors, and a lot of milkshakes besides. As a result, the queue of customers went around the block.[58]

38,000 McDonald's franchises later, every aspect of their business is a finely tuned, repeatable process, designed to minimise time delays and costs, deliver a consistent product and maximise profits. Food is sourced, processed, delivered and prepared exactly the same way every time. Customers drive up to their windows and are served the same way every time. New staff are taken on and trained the same way every time. Marketing campaigns are timed to announce different phases the same way every time. Franchises are sold and contracted the same way every time.

We may or may not admire the product, the company or its values, but we should at least admire their systems thinking. McDonald's has perfected a system for delivering the same experience every time, with occasional minor changes.

What if your business is nothing like that and relies on innovation? The founder of Netflix, Reed Hastings, makes the point that change sometimes comes in tiny slow increments and sometimes in huge rapid leaps. For 5,000 years the horse dominated transport and then in one generation, from 1900 to 1930, it was replaced by the car. It didn't matter how refined or automated your horse-drawn transport business was, you were going to be displaced by a new form of transport.

Reed recognised fairly soon at Netflix, which started as a DVD mailing service, that everything was going to change as the internet and the possibility of streaming movies arrived. He had prior experience with an earlier company, Pure Software, where he tried to dummy proof the systems, only realising too late that then only dummies wanted to work there.[59] At Netflix, he knew he needed flexible thinkers who could redesign things from first principles.

So, processes need to be built as 'horses for courses', so to speak. Where you need highly consistent automated processes, you design them one way. Where you need flexibility to adapt as the humans operating the system see fit, you design them another way. Where do you fit on the continuum from the McDonald's process methods to the Netflix philosophy?

In the early days of manufacturing, with people doing the work that is now so often done by machines, they wanted people to do one thing as well as possible and pass it on to the next person in the production line to do their part, and so on. This was how Henry Ford organised his production line for the model T Ford.[60] However, over several decades, people realised the mind-numbing and disengaging nature of this method.

In the 1970s, Volvo reimagined the production line, by forming work teams who would take one car at a time all the way from beginning to completion. Volvo discovered that workers were happier, productivity and quality improved and so did profits.[61]

Toyota introduced the 'just in time' or lean manufacturing system that delivered parts and other resources, making only what was needed, when it was needed and in the amount needed.[62] They believed that the ideal conditions for making things were created when machines, facilities and people worked together to add value without generating waste.

Tesla cars and the batteries they use are built in gigafactories, designed from the ground up to run on sustainable energy, using robotics to build the cars with assistance from the human workforce. While they have had plenty of teething troubles, they are sticking with their vision of 'machines building machines'.[63]

The hierarchy of business systems

Before jumping into setting up better systems and processes in your business, let's make it clear how they fit
into a chain of consideration. Any system has to serve
a business function. The hierarchy looks like this:

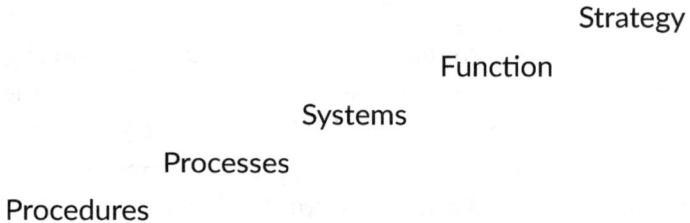

Strategy

Function

Systems

Processes

Procedures

- **Standard operating procedures** should serve
  a process, which forms part of a system, which
  serves a function, which runs to achieve the
  strategic objectives of the business.

- **Processes** are a series of repeated steps, where
  each step may have a standard operating
  procedure.

- **Systems** reflect the combination of processes,
  people, technology and interfaces.

- **Function**, in this context, is meant to describe
  a key chain in the company's business, such as
  marketing or production.

- **Strategy** includes the key principles, values and
  policies of the company.

Systems tend to look at the big picture, while processes refine the steps people take with the tools and integration needed to achieve the system's purpose. A process is usually designed for efficiency, for doing a series of tasks more rapidly, with less wasted time and resources. A system is designed for effectiveness. So, if a process is efficient, but not achieving the overarching goal, that problem needs to be solved at the system level. Sometimes our problems may be caused at a system level beyond our individual businesses at an industry, government or international economic level.

A system can reflect a culture and its values, as well as enforced policies. This is evident in business, in society and in the way different countries operate. You can use system thinking to get a fresh perspective on problems that seem to be local and granular, but may be much bigger – even global.

Astronaut Ron Garan realised, while floating in the International Space Station, how the incredibly thin layer of biosphere surrounding Earth was all there was supporting every living thing, on the only planet we know of with life. He had the insight that the problems of the world need to be looked at; not from an economic, national, societal or any other 'us vs them' framework. There is no 'us vs them' when we use a planetary perspective. Until a critical mass of people adopts a planetary system-first approach, which he believes is coming, we won't solve the numerous problems at any micro level on Earth.[64]

Purpose-driven businesses operate with more aware-ness and hopefully some contribution to a healthier planetary approach. We all use processes and systems every day, but we may not have thought of them fitting together like this. Zooming back into a more focused view of getting our businesses to work at their best, we need to develop a system for every key function in our business.

Core business functions

Nearly every business must fulfil the following functions:

- Create products or services

- Acquire and retain customers

- Produce and deliver

- Engage employees

- Manage finances

- Set direction and strategy

- Provide governance

Often these functions are carried out by departments with traditional titles such as:

- Research and development

- Production

- Marketing

- Sales

- Customer care

- Operations

- Human resources

- Finance

- IT

- CEO office

- Board of directors

- Investor relations

Whether you use traditional titles or not, every business needs a system to fulfil these core functions. With a well-functioning system and accompanying processes you can feel more assured that the key functions will get done, whether you're there or not.

Expert-based founders often get stuck on feeling they can do the core jobs better than anyone else. One of the toughest challenges of a smaller business is to get to the stage where the founder can take significant time off. A good set of systems will allow employees to step in and do what you might have been doing. It'll allow new employees to rapidly get trained and fulfil their roles the way you want them done.

Over a longer period, you probably want to grow the business to the extent it can run without you. That gives you the freedom to take time off or think strategically about developing new assets for this business or the next one. If you want to sell your business, the buyer will want a business that doesn't stop when the founder leaves.

Summary

- Every core function of your business needs a system, so that current and new staff know how to produce a consistent result. Developing these systems is vital to your ability to grow from a Startup into a Scaleup organisation.

- The type of systems and extent of them varies depending on your company's needs and style, whether you're rigorously disciplined or promoting creativity.

- Systems serve your mission and strategy. Within each system you need processes, people, technology and interfaces that make the system not only efficient but effective.

14
How To Create A Process

There are a huge number of apps and software platforms available now for customer relationship management, known as CRMs, that track all communications and nurture relationships with leads and clients. There is also a plethora of enterprise resource planning platforms, known as ERPs, to manage accounting, procurement, project management, supply chain operations and other day-to-day business processes. If you can't find one off the shelf, you can find a development team to design a bespoke solution. But before plonking your company bank card down for one, it's useful to do some thinking and planning on paper first.

Assessing and improving processes

There are several steps in assessing and improving any process in your business.

1. **What is the purpose of the process?** Start with a fresh look at what you want the process to achieve. Do you just need to refine the current process or do you need to design a whole new process, from a blank sheet of paper, with new tech and new methods?

2. **What are the current problems?** Don't fix it if it ain't broken, used to be the mantra most businesses adopted. However, in today's competitive world, the chances are you need to keep improving every aspect of your business.

3. **What is the ideal outcome?** Imagine your new process is now operating. What would that look like and what benefits would you want from it?

4. **What principles and values should govern the process?** In most businesses, but particularly with customer-facing staff, sooner or later they'll come across a situation that isn't covered by the process and standard operating procedures. You'll want them to understand your company values so well they can immediately respond and look after customers appropriately.

5. **Map the current process** Take the time to set out a flow chart from go to whoa, with the main and alternative pathways sketched out. Draft responses to various possible scenarios.

6. **Brainstorm then consider changes** Ask what could be done differently and let the ideas fly for a while without being shot down. Once you've had sufficient time on that side, put on your discernment cap and start selecting what could work better than before.

7. **Map best new processes** Pick one best way, as long as it's feasible, and do another flow chart.

8. **Test it** For an internal process, you can set up a measured test now to see how much or how little it achieves and if it reaches the nominated goal. You may want to show external users a paper or a digital version first, then make your MVP.

9. **Refine or adjust based on feedback** Was it user-friendly? Did it achieve your reasons for doing it, ie, made things cheaper, improved quality, got things done quicker or was more effective?

10. **Implement** When the users and operators are satisfied, the technology is sorted and, where necessary, the new process is interfaced with other processes, you're ready to launch it to your wider audience.

Goals and accountability

A couple of years ago, my wife bought me a Fitbit to gently nudge me into doing a bit more exercise. For the first week I eagerly went out each day to get my recommended goal of 10,000 steps done. It felt good to be out of the office, walking around my neighbourhood and exploring some streets I hadn't been down before, as I found different routes and took a couple of longer walks each day.

The next week I had a work deadline to meet and I only got out about half the days. The following week it was the same, and by the time a month had passed the Fitbit had become more of a fashionable adornment than a tool to get fit. I expect we've all had this experience, battling with the paradox of getting ourselves to do what we know we should.

A few months later, however, an engineering company for which I was a non-exec director, decided to enrol everyone in their company, including the board of directors, into a 'Steptember' team competition. Every team and individual would post their daily number of steps on an internal website and at the end some fun prizes would be given to the winning team.

Suddenly, me and my faulty willpower were on the hook. If I failed to do 10,000 steps a day, I'd be letting down my team and my sins would be visible for all to see. While plenty of the employees did a lot more than 10,000, I managed to at least get that number done, even if it involved making phone calls while I circled the block or pacing the living room floor while watching a show late at night.

> We don't have trouble setting goals, we have trouble creating a way to get them done.

Structures for success

Individuals and teams need a way of ensuring we complete what we start. A framework we willingly commit to that, once joined, is designed to require the behaviour needed to achieve the goal. This often involves the following components:

- A strong reason for doing it

- A public declaration of what you commit to doing

- A method of getting it done and measuring it along the way

- Habitual behaviour patterns to lock in the necessary actions

- Rewards for achieving both the end result and steps along the way

- Perceived pain, or postponed benefits, for not achieving the steps en route

- A buddy, coach or support network to encourage and hold you accountable

Objectives and Key Results

One of the better ways of achieving goals at work is a system originally laid out by Andy Gove at Intel called Objectives and Key Results (OKRs). Andy realised, as had the original Business Management guru Peter Drucker, that what gets measured gets done.[65]

The method has you choosing a vitally important company objective and then considering what Key Results would have to be achieved along the way to reaching the objective.

There is a distinction between Key Results and Tasks, which can cause confusion if not clearly understood. Let's say your objective is to grow sales and profit without overstressing the team. Tasks that might be needed to achieve that could include:

- Holding a meeting with staff to discuss and decide sales targets

- Modelling cash flow budgets to assess new staff hiring timing and numbers

- Advertising for new staff

- Selecting and onboarding new staff members

- Increasing sales by 10% over the quarter, while holding costs below a 3% increase

Not all of these are Key Results. In fact, as stated above, only the last one – increasing sales by 10% over the quarter – is one. Key Results need to be metrics showing progress, over or under targets, on the way to achieving the main objective.

One-off activities, like holding a meeting to discuss and decide targets or selecting a new staff member, are not ongoing metrics. They are important tasks that are necessary, but by this methodology they are Tasks listed underneath the metric of a Key Result.

Reordering things would look like this:

Objective

Grow sales and profits without overstressing the team.

Key Result 1: Increase staff engagement, including well-being, by 10% over three months.

Task a) Meet with staff to cocreate a hiring plan.

Task b) Provide incentives for behaviour in line with the objective and company values.

Task c) Have staff plan integration and training of new staff.

Task d) Provide work flexibility and implement a well-being programme.

Key Result 2: Increase sales by 10% over the next quarter, while holding costs below a 3% increase.

Task a) Model cash flow outcomes of options for hiring plan.

Task b) Advertise for new staff.

Task c) Select and train new staff.

Task d) Review sales conversations weekly for continuing improvement.

At the task level, you need to nominate who is responsible for each one, by what dates they need to be completed and what resources are required.

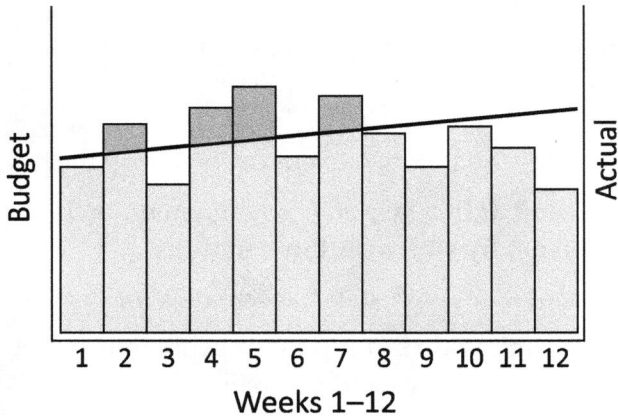

Tracking actual sales vs budget

Using this method of OKRs, everyone can see a straightforward visualisation of whether the team is winning, holding water or losing. It provides an intrinsic motivation to make progress and solve whatever problems or obstacles there might be in the way. People will want to see that line on the chart trending up.

A traffic light system is a further useful visual aid, eg, green to indicate above target progress, yellow for on track and red for below target. A traffic light dashboard is also a great way for department heads to track the progress of each member of their team for any other task. It's a quick and easy way to stay on top of a lot of information that otherwise would clog up your mental bandwidth.

The four disciplines of execution

Another wrinkle on ways to get things done is known as the Four Disciplines of Execution (4DX), developed by Chris McChesney, Sean Covey and Jim Huling from the Franklin Covey group,[66] famous for the book with the irresistible title, *The 7 Habits of Highly Effective People*.[67]

Every new methodology has to have a cute name, so they call your main objective your Wildly Important Goal (WIG).

Discipline 1 Pick a WIG that the whole organisation can contribute to.

Discipline 2 Choose the lag indicator to measure.

Discipline 3 Choose the lead indicators that are precursors to achieving results and measure, track and display progress. These indicators should be things the team members can influence.

Discipline 4 Set up a cadence of accountability conversations where team members report on progress, discuss any issues and commit to what they'll do next.

The 4DX method is designed to have your team lift their sights from what they call the whirlwind, and focus attention and effort on one vital initiative.

Summary

- Develop and refine your processes by first defining their purpose and the principles that will guide them before creating a flow chart to test and implement them.

- Once you have freely committed to a goal, design a structure for success that locks you into completing what you've promised to do.

- Use systems like OKRs and 4DX to set up ways to ensure your team achieves the most important objectives that will make a difference.

15
Personal Effectiveness

Time management

Every founder complains that they don't have *enough* hours in the day. However, what they need is *more effective* use of those hours.

Consider that Elon Musk and Richard Branson don't have any more hours in the day than you do. They probably just don't spend them the same way you do. Of course, they have way more staff and resources, and they may be supermen, but the point is as your organisation grows in size – and indeed to enable it to grow in size – you need to shift what you do with those hours.

In the early stages of your company, you're doing everything and that's the way it must be. Even as you acquire staff, it's common for the founder to still be spending most of their hours in operational matters; things like meeting potential customers, closing sales, fine-tuning and delivering the service, handling any stuff ups, chasing accounts and solving lots of little problems that the staff bring to you, as they know you'll have the answer.

'Well, of course,' you might be thinking, 'what else would I be doing?' Well, you need to judge which of those things needs to be done by you. Some still will, if your assessment or expertise is fundamental to the business outcome, however you need to give up quite a lot of those operational tasks and spend more time in significant uninterrupted blocks of time on strategic considerations.

To make the shift from the Startup phase through the Setup phase and on to the Scaleup phase requires you to stop spending your time keeping a lot of urgent plates spinning every day. You'll need to hire and train others to spin those plates and be willing to see some plates get broken along the way.

The bigger your organisation gets, the more time you need to spend on longer-term strategic matters that will move the needle. You need to be contemplating the future you want for your company and how to get there, rather than chasing every urgency to get through another hectic day.

Write down how many hours a week you currently spend in each of these blocks of activities:

- Holding meetings
- Dealing with staff issues
- Solving other random problems

- Sales
- Delivery
- Accounts

- Hiring and onboarding new staff
- Training and developing all staff
- Designing staff engagement and reward plans

- Setting budgets
- Implementing goal metric tracking and accountability
- Monitoring and leading the performance standards for staff
- Developing and refining systems
- Marketing

- Contemplating the future of your industry

- Innovating new products or services

- Defining and communicating vision, mission and values

- Considering the strategy for growth

- Defining your brand and its voice

Did you find that most of your time was taken up in the upper sections of that list, with little or no time spent on the matters near the bottom of the list? What would happen if you tipped the list upside down and spent more time on the currently neglected sections?

The transition

You have to let other people run the day-to-day business as you spend time on the things that make your business grow for the future. You have to give up being the expert and hire other experts, while you become a true CEO.

Now one of the problems is that the skills and knowledge that made you an expert are not the skills and knowledge – or at least not the only ones – that make you a good CEO. If your business is growing, or if you are committed to getting it to grow faster, you have a choice to make. Are you going to shift your time and focus to the work of a CEO or are you going to remain the expert and hire someone else to be, at least, the general manager? The latter choice is viable, if being the expert is what gives you joy and your operational time in that role is irreplaceable as the growth engine of the business. You'd still be the owner, but now you'd have someone else as the manager or CEO.

David Ogilvy founded the groundbreaking advertising agency Ogilvy & Mather. Later in life he decided he'd rather be the creative director than the CEO. He realised he wasn't a very good manager or administrator and that the creative role was what he loved most and where he could make the greatest impact for the company.[68]

Not everyone wants to make the shift from expert to entrepreneur, as it involves taking on a range of responsibilities and activities rather different from being the expert. It can be stressful if you don't change the way you go about it. As CEO, you need to start thinking and operating from a different point of view and spend your time on strategic matters in decent blocks of time.

Time blocking

One effective way of doing this is to make appointments for yourself in your diary, of at least two hours at a time, to get some thinking and planning done on matters like the vision, strategy or other matters needing time to consider.

It helps to take half an hour on a Friday or the weekend and sit down somewhere pleasant with a coffee to look at your calendar two weeks out. List the strategic thinking projects you need to complete and book some decent time in your calendar. Then treat them as inviolate appointments, as unchangeable and as uninterruptable as you would an appointment with your biggest customer.

Unless we follow a process like this, the day-to-day urgent fracas fills every hour and there's no time left for things that can change the game.

Routines and habits

In 2022, Ingo Willuhn and researchers from the Netherlands Institute for Neuroscience trained rats over ten weeks in a seeking and taking task, resulting in habitual seeking behaviour. Rats were trained to press a lever to seek food and then another lever to get a food pellet. They found dopamine levels spiked in the dorsomedial striatum in the basal ganglia when these rats pressed the seek lever initiating the process, reinforcing the habit that led, after the other lever was pressed, to getting food. To test the validity of this finding, they directly stimulated dopamine neurons in this same ancient part of the brain and instantly promoted seeking behaviour and habit formation.[69] Other studies in monkeys have shown that dopamine is released more in anticipation than completion of a reward and that a greater dose of dopamine is released if there is only a 50% chance of the reward being delivered.[70]

In mice and men, we're driven to install and repeat habitual behaviour by our internal biochemical dopamine factory.[71] Habits are a dopamine-driven feedback loop.[72] While this may sound rather grim and deterministic, it's best we acknowledge it, learn to control it when needed and use it in a positive manner for what we really want to achieve.

To be significantly successful in business, you probably have to be a bit obsessive about it. Otherwise, you may not get through all the barriers and create something that can make a real impact. The trick is not to give up addictive-like behaviours entirely, but to recognise the unhelpful ones and install helpful ones.

If, for example, you find you're thrown to solve every problem yourself rather than allowing your staff to struggle to solve them, even though you know that's not helpful, you have ingrained a habit that's become a racket. To get yourself to kick a habit like this takes recognising the dopamine hit you get that appeals to you, and also recognising what not kicking it is costing you. Generally, you only give this kind of thing up when you realise in your gut how much it's harming what you want – a fully functional team that can free up your time to spend with your family and on more strategic and creative thinking.

The habit you would want to install in this example, is to say no to all enquiries from employees asking you to solve a problem, or how to solve a problem they could eventually solve themselves. Accept that they'll make mistakes but they'll learn from them and do better next time. More importantly, they'll learn a new habit of tackling problems themselves.

You might want to cue up your new habit by writing the response you want to make, like, 'No, you're the one to solve it, not me', on a card. Place it in plain sight on your desk. Often to get a new habit started you need something to remind you at the time of what it should be, until with enough repetition it becomes a habit itself. Every time you follow the new process the way you want to, put a tick in your diary and give yourself a high five or some other form of recognition that you're winning. The only exception to this should be something that's mission critical, a genuine crisis, in which case you need to step in and lead the process of overcoming it, even if it's your employees who have to do the work.

Changing habits is a big topic, and for a detailed treatise I recommend reading *Atomic Habits* by James Clear.[73]

Stress and burnout

At least some level of stress is a fairly constant accompaniment if you're ambitious for what your company can do. They say if you don't have any challenges, you're just not pursuing a big enough mission.

There's a difference between stress and burnout, and the latter is not just an extension of the former.[74] When you're stressed, you are still on the job. You may be anxious, but you're actively chasing down issues with energy and some success and, while you feel under pressure, you're still hopeful of completing your tasks. A decent holiday usually helps.

Burnout is different. You may be withdrawing from work and perhaps from people, starting to doubt if you can complete what you want to and even questioning if it's all worth it. You might start to feel depressed.[75] A holiday won't fix this.

While an overwhelming feeling of having too much to do can be part of being burned out, I've observed there's often something else going on. You may have become disheartened by the lack of care and commitment of some of your employees or of other stakeholders. You've grown fed up with them and have given up hope of them acting the way you think they should, by the values you yourself live by and have tried to install in your team.

If this is the case, you may paradoxically be too nice. You let your employees get away with things where they should not, or give people who should be sacked too many second chances. You may not have spelt out in crystal-clear terms the values and standards you expect your employees to observe at work, or you may have avoided what seems to you like a confrontational conversation with someone with a more naturally dominant personality.

At the end of the day, this is your baby and you have the most at stake. It's time to take a stand, bite the bullet and make things clear – crystal clear. Set out a code of conduct and make it plain that you expect people to follow it and there will be consequences if they don't. The relief you feel when you do will be better than a holiday. But if burnout persists, seek professional help. Your own oxygen mask needs to go on first.

Summary

- You can't get any more hours in the day, but you can spend them more wisely on things that leverage the future progress of the company, while allowing others to deal with the daily whirlwind.

- We form our habits, then our habits shape our future, unless we audit them. Make a commitment to change and set up triggers to remind and direct those changes.

- We may not be able to avoid stress, but we can avoid or deal with burnout by insisting other people meet the values and standards required, while seeking help for ourselves, or others with burnout, when necessary.

SPRINGBOARD 5
PROMOTION

Build a marketing machine

The Australian male lyrebird possesses a magnificent feathered tail, which it vibrates over the head of the female hen while dancing backwards during mating rituals, on one of up to twenty mounds it builds in the bush for this purpose. It's another extraordinary capability that adds an extra layer of persuasion to their elaborate courtship of the opposite sex.

Male lyrebirds have a unique ability to mimic not only other birds but also virtually any sound they hear, such as squeaking trees, camera shutters, car alarms, human voices and even chain saws. They also have the ability to mimic the panicked alarm calls of a mixed flock of birds – a sound they only use during mating, or if a female is attempting to leave the mound without mating.[76] In effect, it appears they use it to tell the hen they're better off here with them, rather than venturing away from the mound where other dangers might be lurking.

Marketing has been around for a long, long time.

16
Marketing 101

Today's methods of marketing may be new but the principles are timeless. Find a potential customer and take them on a journey of discovery, demonstrating that you and your product or service will give them an outcome they want, even if they didn't know they wanted it before you arrived.

Marketing's three essential steps

1. **Emotion** We like to think of ourselves as what economists call 'rational actors', but while we mostly act in our own interests, it's as emotional actors first. Even in business dealings we're prompted initially by emotion. The word emotion suggests 'e', as in energy, prompting motion: e-motion.

The set-up is that we already want something or are frustrated by a problem, though we may need prompting to realise it. If we then come across some marketing and we instinctively feel (notice I said feel) it might solve that desire or problem, then we'll investigate further. Without some emotional connection, we usually won't bother.

2. **Logic** Having had our interest piqued, we then become more analytical and seek validation or justification for our impending decision, or in some cases a decision we've already made. Will it do the job? Is it a better solution than the alternatives? Do we trust the organisation and the people? Is it a good deal? And so on. This may take several contact points over some time.

3. **Fear of loss** Even having connected emotionally and deciding rationally that a particular product or service is right, we can still procrastinate and not get around to actually buying it. In 2002, psychologist Daniel Kahneman was awarded the Nobel prize in economics for his work with Amos Tversky, which showed people are more emotionally invested in avoiding a loss than making a gain.[77] Often it takes a form of FOMO (fear of missing out), like a limited-time offer or the original problem becoming unavoidably urgent so we fear we won't control it, to get us to close the deal.[78]

The buying process

The buying process can differ, depending on whether you or the seller is the seeker.

As a buyer, if you already know you want something, you tend to rapidly go consciously or unconsciously through these steps to find a solution you want, in terms acceptable to you. For example, if you know you want a TV you might go to a retailer with a big range and talk with a salesperson about your desired features and budget. You may well have done a fair bit of looking online and go in with specific brands and features in mind. If the salesperson is any good, they'll ask you a few more questions to understand what will satisfy you and show you some alternatives. Then they'll probably pitch one a bit more expensive than your budget, with some extra benefits. If it appeals, you'll stretch your budget and buy it on the spot. On the other hand, you might shop online, make your own choice and get it delivered. In this scenario, whether in store or online, the vendor relies on their brand reputation, marketing messages, product information and the deal offered.

If, on the other hand, you're having trouble getting to sleep at night, you may not have any specific solution in mind, or even know there is a solution. In this case, you won't go looking for a product, so now it's up to a company with a solution to connect with you in some way; first to communicate a solution exists and then

STARTUP, SCALEUP OR SCREWUP

to persuade you to buy it. This is likely to take more steps, with multiple contacts, before a sale is made. From the company's perspective they need to decide who their most likely buyer is and figure out where to find them, then how to pitch a new product and progress to a sale.

Breaking that down into smaller steps, as a marketer your tasks are to:

1. Introduce yourself to someone you want to have as a client

2. Understand their existing thoughts and feelings, pains and desires

3. Help them realise they have an underlying want or problem that can be solved

4. Pitch an outcome that emotionally appeals to them

5. Explain in rational terms how you provide a comprehensive solution

6. Provide some evidence you can deliver it, and explain why they should choose you

7. Continue adding value, building relationships and trust

8. De-risk the deal and limit the time available

9. Re-emphasise the emotional outcome you deliver

10. Make an irresistible offer

The marketing journey is the same but the avenues are changing. Traditionally, you had a choice of print, radio, TV or outdoor billboards. The digital world has opened up many different options, each with their own pros and cons: Google, Facebook, Instagram, YouTube, Tik-Tok, Twitter, LinkedIn… and no doubt more to come.

You can pay to advertise on these platforms, or you can pursue unpaid organic connections. How do you choose which platform to use?

The fundamental principle should be to go where your niche of customers hang out the most. As gentleman robber Willie Sutton said in 1952, when asked why he robbed banks, 'Because that's where the money is.'[79]

Whichever platform you choose, paid ads can pay off if you have a strong value proposition for a discrete audience who badly want to solve a problem. Lead-generation systems are often advertised on Facebook, because they know a lot of early-stage entrepreneurs and small businesses desperately need more leads. If they're not already searching for them, they're triggered by the appeal of more leads, if the ad makes a big promise, with a new twist.

The initial challenge if you do pursue paid advertising is competing with the wall of noise that assaults us daily, in order to cut through and get noticed. In a sense, your greatest competition is *not* other companies in your industry. Your fight is with every form of information and entertainment competing for that rarest of commodities – the undivided attention of your desired audience.

Websites

Your website is central to modern marketing for one or both of these purposes:

- A place for potential customers to check your credentials
- A place to begin a connected journey to sales

If your customers are high-ticket businesses, you may only need the former, where you show your capabilities and thought leadership. If your customers are small businesses or consumers, it will help to set your website up a little differently, for example so you can offer a high-value PDF in exchange for opting-in with their name and email.

One of the more effective ways to start the journey for potential customers is to offer them a tantalising high-value download for free as an opt-in, but do it based on a psychologically sound strategy. For example, if you were an accounting firm, as a lead-generation article you might want to write up a report about a series of steps to make the most of your tax return. A better strategy would be to write it up as a series of mistakes to avoid and give it an attention-grabbing headline, like 'How to avoid the five most common tax planning disasters even smart professionals can make.' Inside the article, after pointing out the problems, you would go on to include the same material that would have gone into the purely positive pitch, but it now has greater impact and is more likely to lead to further conversations. In most situations, pain (or the potential for pain) is a stronger motivator than gain (or the potential for gain).

Search engine optimisation

Search engine optimisation (SEO) is a specialised field that I am far from expert in, so I won't say much other than giving some framing that might be useful.

There's an ongoing struggle between Google attempting to make search rankings useful and reasonable, and smart developers and SEO strategists attempting to beat the system, either with so-called white hat or black hat methods. The long-term path to page one ranking is to become an authority in your field, post regular thought-leading articles and have other respected people and websites acknowledge your authority.

One of the more challenging aspects for most business owners is not only creating thought-leadership articles but also doing it sufficiently regularly to have an impact on Google rankings. Some people outsource this work to journalists or media agencies, after providing some guidelines and insights, then editing what they produce.

Another method is opening up through artificial intelligence (AI). There are now programmes that will automatically write articles for you, based on the kind of input you would brief a journalist with. ChatGPT is one of these programs, developed by Open AI. While you may think an AI auto-written article would be just rubbish, it's rapidly improving and is likely to be of help, if set up and edited appropriately. I suspect Google will do their best to penalise the black hat idea of having the AI app write and post twenty articles a day for you as a fast track to page one rankings. Google themselves are working on their own AI search tool, nicknamed Bard, to counter the Microsoft-backed ChatGPT and AI enhanced Bing. The rapid emergence of AI as a search and writing tool is a major innovation that risks disrupting the current Google business model.

One other note of caution; check your chances of ever reaching page one before blowing your budget trying. Some search terms are so popular only the biggest companies can get there. In that case, you're better to buy Google Ads and show up above or below the organic content when someone types in a key phrase they might use in your industry.

Thought leadership

In the long term, you might get a decent bang for your buck with posts you don't have to pay for, but underline long term and add regular – and interesting.

People like Gary Vaynerchuk, who morphed from posting online about the wines his family company carried to become a leading guru about social media, will tell you to post five times a day. He can point to how he has a following of millions with several hundred comments each time he posts, to which in his early days he replied to every single one.[80] Recognise that doing that has become his business, and it's not yours. Your challenge, unless you outsource it (which is possible) is to post something more than a self-congratulatory corporate post; something with some actual thought behind it that will be of real interest and help. Do it consistently a couple of times a week.

What you might do in the realm of social influencing, on Instagram for example, is beyond my ken.

PR

Elon Musk says companies shouldn't spend their money on advertising but rather on product development – or as he puts it in engineering terms, on signal, not noise.[81]

That's fine, but Tesla doesn't need advertising because Elon does such a great job of promotion via his prominent presence on social media, like Twitter, and frequent media interviews and speeches. In fact, as you probably know, he liked Twitter so much he bought the company, so now he has his very own media platform to do his bidding and keep his name and projects in the limelight. He also attracts global attention with his stunts, like launching a Tesla roadster into space. All of this is, in fact, marketing, which Elon no doubt realises, despite his protestations.

Richard Branson is another expert user of PR and appearances to promote his businesses. Whether it's flying around the world in a hot air balloon, or floating into Sydney Harbour on a fake iceberg, Richard has mastered the art of getting the world's media to publicise his businesses much more cost effectively than using paid advertising.[82]

While you may not have such stunts in mind (but so much the better if you do), you can probably do more with PR than you think. Media of all kinds live and breathe on content and if you have an interesting story they think will appeal to their audience, they'll give you a go. The trick is to write a press release with the audience in mind, not yourself. Don't just launch into your products and services and how great they are. Write up a piece with insight into an industry problem, or with a personal angle, or something a little controversial. Then tag on how your product or service fits in at the end.

Of course, one of the other groups desperate for content are podcasts and these are even easier to get on, if you have half an interesting story. In all cases, tell a story.

Summary

- A customer's first trigger to buy is likely to be an emotional feeling, followed by checking the logic of their choice, but often they'll only sign up when they urgently need it or fear they'll lose the chance.

- Put your ads or free content on the social media platform your customers are already on.

- Set your website up for its purpose, as a credibility showcase, a lead-generation tool or both. Most business owners will need expert advice on SEO to assess if it's worth spending money on, and if it is, how to do it cost effectively.

- Gradually build a following with some thoughtful, useful, preferably entertaining posts.

- When you have a story to tell, you can usually get some free publicity.

17
Intrinsic Brand Value

Afew years ago, my wife and I went on a holiday to Bali and stayed at a hotel near the seafront. We arrived late afternoon and the next morning went for a walk along the beach. There we were met by an enthusiastic purveyor of premium horological devices. He showed us some fine examples of well-known brands, such as Rolex, Longines, Omega, TAG Heuer and others. After some haggling, I bought a Rolex for about $20 and wondered how it was possible I'd saved myself some $5,000 that I would expect to pay. OK, I knew it was fake, but it got me thinking about the value we ascribe to some products and brands.

CASE STUDY: ROLLS-ROYCE

You may know that Rolls-Royce these days is actually made by BMW.[83] It so happens that the premium BMW cars share a similar platform, engines and other components with Rolls-Royce. To quite a large extent, the luxury BMW models have the same capability as the Rolls-Royce, but the Rolls-Royce costs three times as much. The difference is intrinsic brand value. As good as the BMW product is, a Rolls-Royce has some perceived intangible extra appeal that allows them to charge that much more. In fact, intangible assets like the name and logo of Rolls-Royce have turned out to be as valuable as its tangible assets, such as the facilities where the cars were manufactured.

In 1998, Vickers decided to sell Rolls-Royce Motors. The most likely buyer was BMW, which already supplied engines and other components for Rolls-Royce and Bentley cars, but BMW's final offer of £340 million was beaten by Volkswagen's offer of £430 million. Vickers plc sold the vehicle designs, nameplates, administrative headquarters, production facilities, Spirit of Ecstasy, and Rolls-Royce grille shape trademarks to Volkswagen AG.

However, Rolls-Royce Holdings plc, the aero-engine maker, retained certain essential trademarks, including the Rolls-Royce brand name and logo, and they decided to license them to BMW. That was a level nine screwup and, as you might imagine, caused some fuss. Volkswagen wanted the Rolls-Royce name and BMW wanted to manufacture the cars. After some time, they negotiated a settlement whereby Volkswagen made the cars with a licence from BMW to use the name until 2003, and thereafter BMW took over manufacturing.[84]

If you can create a brand with intrinsic value above and beyond the commodity value of similar products or services, you're likely to reap several benefits:

- Greater profit margins
- Customer loyalty
- Rapid take-up of new products or services

You don't have to necessarily operate at the super-expensive end of things to grow profits. It's useful to think about where you are on a curve, from something that's a pure commodity that has to be priced competitively to something that's a pure brand, where the intellectual property, the intrinsic value, enables you to make a profit beyond the functional value of the product. Whereabouts are you on this spectrum?

If you're successful and selling in reasonable numbers at the luxury end of the market, it's likely to be very profitable. If you're successful at being the cheapest, providing the greatest range and the most convenient service, the margins will be a lot less so you'll need a lot more volume, but ultimately there's good profit at this end of the spectrum too.

Customers will develop loyalty for a brand at the cheap end of the market if they perceive other benefits.

CASE STUDY: BUNNINGS

From its humble beginnings in 1886, when brothers Arthur and Robert Bunning opened their first hardware store in Perth, the company has gone Australia-wide and become a retail giant, stocking a huge range of home handyman and trade brands in giant no-frills barnlike buildings. Bunnings has stayed true to its roots, consistently offering high levels of service, value and experience at the lowest prices – guaranteed. They're known for their sausage sizzles outside and friendly staff inside, who feature in homespun, easy-going ads developed by Trinity Fredricks of Strawberry Media, who later became a client of mine. Offering the convenience of a large store with a friendly family and community focus has made Bunnings Australia's most trusted brand.[85]

Woolworths spent many billions setting up sixty-three Masters stores, attempting to compete, but ultimately failed and closed. This was largely because they didn't have any positive differentiation and couldn't shake the warm appeal of Bunnings to its loyal tribe of customers.[86] If your claim is being second cheapest, you'll probably struggle.

Traditionally, the middle area on this spectrum is a tough place to generate much profit in, but it can be done. If you're in-between, you need an edge to succeed, such as being a clearly superior product at affordable prices.

If you can provide value for money with a fabulous product, your payoff can be the greater market share you capture, and hence a growing business, even though the profit margin may not be as large.

How do you create intrinsic value? In essence, the way to achieve this is by obsessively developing greater and greater products and services for a targeted niche area of passionate customers. By producing insanely complete and remarkable solutions, you too may be rewarded by a queue of customers around the block or sold-out signs on the door.

Pricing

Many business owners are reluctant to put their prices up, fearing they'll lose customers as their willingness to pay declines. It depends on the industry, but in many cases they probably could charge more and come out ahead with more profit, even if they lose a percentage of customers.

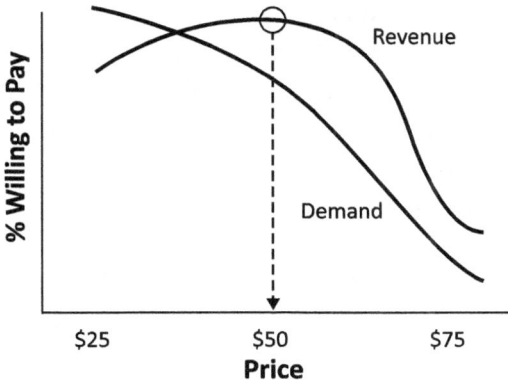

Finding the optimum price for maximum revenue

The way the maths works, if your gross profit margin is 40%, you can lose 20% of your customers after increasing your prices by 10% and still make the same profit. Chances are you won't lose as many as 20% of your customers, so you come out well ahead.

If your gross profit margin is worse, let's say 20%, then putting your prices up works even better. In this case you would have to lose 33% of your customers after a 10% price increase to make only the same profit as before. In fact, the worse your profit margin is, the more compelling it is to raise your prices. If your profit margin is only 10%, for a 10% price rise to be a mistake, you would have to lose more than an astonishing 50% of your customers.[87]

Putting your prices up may be the simplest and quickest way to increase your profits. This is even more the case if your product or service happens to be price inelastic, as contrasted with the more usual price elastic situation. An example of a relatively price inelastic product is oil. In 1974, the Saudi oil minister, Sheikh Yamani (pronounced like 'shake yourmoney') wondered if we would still buy their oil if they put the price up by 400%.[88] It turned out we would. We may not like higher petrol prices but our usage doesn't drop off much, since we consider it essential.

There is a further type of product or service, known as Veblen goods, named after the economist Thorstein Veblen who coined the term 'conspicuous consumption'.

With these products, demand actually increases as prices go up.[89] Luxury products like high-end handbags, designer jewellery, yachts, supercars, watches and cosmetics are in this happy space (happy for the makers, that is) where the intrinsic value is tied up with exclusivity and price, at least up to a point.

Brand personality

A company's brand, or product brand, lives in the mind of your customers. Literally.

Michael Platt, the professor of marketing and neuroscience at Wharton, set up an experiment to see directly what was going on in our minds when we engage with well-known brands. Michael and his team used MRI machines to observe the brains of Apple and Samsung users while they heard good, bad and neutral news about their brands. The brain scans of Apple users showed positive reactions when they heard good news about Apple and vice versa when it was negative. The scans of Samsung users, however, were neutral when listening to any kind of news about Samsung and only showed a positive reaction when they heard negative news about Apple. In other words, customers buy Apple for their warm connection with the brand and customers buy Samsung because they hate Apple.[90]

We anthropomorphise brands, meaning we endow them with human qualities. Then we identify with the brands we think represent ourselves, or perhaps more honestly with how we would like ourselves to be perceived. They become part of our identity.

Apple is known for being creative, for being different; McDonald's for family friendliness and convenience; Harley-Davidson for being rebellious; FedEx for reliability; Tiffany & Co for luxury; Nike for determination, outdoor activities and getting on with it; Bunnings for being a friendly place to chat about hardware; Carlton United Breweries for larrikin mateship; Vinomofo for cool wine vibes, without the highbrow bullshit.

Notice how consistent they are with the personalities of their brands in their marketing. They've figured out their desired image, to reflect their customers' values and self-image. They know the feeling they want to evoke and they're focused with their messaging. It doesn't change, and there's no need for it to change. Consistent branding helps cement a feeling of bonding and belonging that results in loyalty, repeat business and an improved profit margin.

Professor Michael Platt has studied the neurological basis of how we decide which brand to buy. He says the battle for business growth does not take place online or on store shelves, but rather in the subconscious mind of the prospective customer. The key to changing preferences is 'the expansion of a brand's positive associations in customers' memories to the point it becomes an automatic, involuntary choice'.[91]

What positive associations and personality do you want to project for your business with your products and services?

Summary

- If you can build intrinsic brand value so that customers will pay more for your product than a commodity-like equivalent, you'll also benefit with extra demand and loyalty.

- Build that intrinsic value by making insanely great stuff that clicks with your tribe.

- You can probably put your prices up without damaging your profits, even if you lose a few customers.

- Think about the personality you want to express as your brand that reflects your ideal customer's value and self-image and, once fashioned, stick with it.

18
Generating Leads

Inbound outbound

The aim of marketing is to find and connect with the kind of people and companies that make up your ideal clients and take them on a journey to a sale.

This can be done by reaching out to potential leads or running a campaign to have them reach out to you. Clearly, most of us would prefer the latter, where we imagine sitting back and watching a stream of candidates knocking on our door, asking for the privilege of being our customer. Making that happen should be a long-term goal for you, but how?

Potential customers need to move through these steps:

- Unaware to aware

- No interest to curious

- 'Can you help me?' to 'Yes, I believe you can'

- 'Can I trust you?' to 'Yes, I can'

- 'Are you the best for me?' to 'Yes, you are'

- 'Do you tick my boxes?' to 'Yes, you do'

- 'Is it a good deal?' to 'Yes, it is'

Marketing funnels vs pipelines

The traditional marketing funnel is based on the idea of selecting the few from the masses. Beginning with a message that's seen by a large number of potential customers, leading to a series of contacts where people who aren't interested in your offer drop out. In addition, weeding out people you don't want to have for customers. You hope to eventually lead to a small percentage of sales at the end of the funnel.

This approach, if done well – let's make that very well – can work if you're after a relatively high volume of leads.

As a paid social media strategy, it could look like this:

1. An ad with a cut-through headline, offering a free, high-value educational PDF to download.

2. Those who accept fill in their name and email and are then sent the PDF as well as being taken to a landing page offering a next-level value item, such as a free strategy session.

3. Those who take that up are asked to fill out a short questionnaire about their business, which weeds out unqualified leads.

4. Those who make it through this step are taken to an automated calendar where they can see available times and immediately confirm a strategy appointment.

5. On the appointment they're provided real value and, if appropriate, offered the opportunity to become a client.

Instead of a PDF it might be a webinar that for three-quarters of the time offers real value and, in the last quarter, pitches a course with a special to take it up only available on the day or a link to follow up for more information.

Obviously, there's going to be a considerable drop off at each stage, but it has the benefit of ending up with appointments with people who have jumped through some hoops to show they have genuine interest. It can be linked with a sequence of emails that follow up those who don't immediately accept with a limited-time offer stacked with bonuses that will disappear after a certain date, triggering the FOMO to get people to act.

The sequence should move from a free offer to an inexpensive offer, before going on to offer the main product at a price that makes a profit. The point of an inexpensive 'coffee or lunch money' offer is that once someone has bought something from you, they are far more likely to go on to become a paying customer at the full price. It's ideal if you can provide the inexpensive offer at a small profit margin that can go back into the marketing budget, though even if it's a loss leader, it's a worthwhile step towards a profitable customer.

The mass market funnel may work in business-to-consumer (B2C) fast-moving consumer markets or with some small businesses, however it's not the best approach in business-to-business (B2B) markets. In these cases, a narrow-targeted pipeline can be a lot more efficient. Everyone says they want leads. What we really need are deals.

CASE STUDY: MERCHGIRLS

Like many businesses, Merchgirls got customers by a range of methods, from repeats to referrals and marketing. We had worked out together that their most profitable customers were going to be large orders, which logically come from large companies. How do you get in the door of large busy companies when you're a much smaller and still relatively unknown company?

As they grew, Merchgirls employed account managers to step in to do the outreach that in the early days they did themselves. Hannah and Pippa tasked them with reaching out to key contacts in high-profile companies that Merchgirls thought would be a great fit for their service. They did it using LinkedIn, coupled with a clever method of demonstrating just how superior their merch was using 'Merch Kits'. LinkedIn has some upgrade options that allow you to search for people in certain positions, by industry, size of company, location and other factors. Their process was as follows:

1. Send a friendly direct message to connect with several people within the marketing department of targeted companies.
2. Ask them if they'd like a free 'Merch Kit' (sample set) that demonstrates what could be done for their company.
3. Send a highly attractive sample kit that is perceived as superior and valuable.
4. Phone them to ask if the sample arrived and if they'd like to see a Menu (catalogue).
5. Send the Menu.
6. Follow up with a phone call to assess interest and request a meeting.
7. Meet to discuss possible order.
8. Take order and onboard as a client.

If they don't become clients, they're nurtured over time with more information and new menus when they come out.

Using this method, after a short period of time, Merchgirls were able to generate leads from 9.1% of the people they approached and converted 43.1% of those leads into customers. As a result of this, they're now getting 45% of new customers this way and it looks like it can scale up from there.

The Merchgirls were using one of the most powerful forms of influence; that of reciprocity, drawing on our innate pull to repay a gift in some way, either to return a generosity or avoid feeling guilty or obligated.

Robert Cialdini wrote about six primary drivers in his classic book, *Influence*, and later added a seventh:

1. Reciprocity – people will return a favour.

2. Commitment – once you've made a commitment, you're more likely to make more.

3. Social proof – people follow what others do or recommend.

4. Authority – people trust authorities.

5. Liking – people are more likely to deal with people they like.

6. Scarcity – people will want things that are rare, or at risk of disappearing.

7. Unity – people want to feel part of a community.[92]

Using these elements in your communication sequences can help move potential customers along the path to becoming clients, with one proviso. It needs to be done in a way that actually serves the best interests of the customer or it will be seen as manipulative and trigger a reflex rejection.

Your marketing funnel – or better, your targeted pipeline – can begin with traditional media, digital media, networking, personal referrals or anywhere else. In each case, the goal is to take them from first contact to an eventual sales conversation in a planned and measured sequence.

Arrow Health runs an addiction rehab hospital and live-in facility that provides leading research-based programmes that CEO Toby Lawrence calls 'The School of Second Chances'. Their pipeline begins with radio ads, inviting people to call them for a confidential conversation. The callers might be addicts themselves, their families or a health professional. The person taking the call takes some details and either passes them on to the appropriate person for a conversation or invites them to accept some educational material by mail. Arrow Health tracks where they come from to assess the effectiveness of their radio ads.

Scorecard marketing

We know people will resist an immediate attempt to sell them your product or service, unless they're already warmed up. A better approach is to offer them something free and low-risk, which they'll value as an educational opportunity. Rather than an education about you and your subject matter, offer them a chance to get educated about themselves.

This can be done with scorecard marketing, a variation on older quiz-based engagement, developed by Daniel Priestley and Glenn Carlson and now available as Scoreapp.[93] The concept is to create a list of questions about your potential client's current capability in an area relevant to your solution. As people answer your questions, they're revealing to you and themselves a more objective insight into how advanced or not they are in that area.

People like to answer quizzes and find out more about their own situation. A quiz can be designed for a wide range of businesses. For example, it might be used as a lead gen tool for accountants, with a quiz that assesses how well a small business owner understands how to reduce their taxes, manage their cash flow and measure their return on capital. Small business owners doing the quiz would be sent their score, along with some tips on how to improve in the areas they need it. This can be an automated yet tailored response that varies based on their particular answers. Along with their summary score, an invite can be emailed to book an appointment for a deeper dive into the meaning of the answers for their business, with a one-to-one discussion that may lead to becoming a client.

There are many choices of how you could set up a pipeline. If one isn't working and after some refinement it still doesn't work, learn what you can from it and try a different path.

Measure your results

Once you have sorted out your pipeline and run it for a while, you should measure the overall effectiveness and the conversion rates at each step to fine-tune its efficiency. A useful ratio is the cost of acquisition to lifetime value. Measure the lifetime value to you of an average customer that comes this way, or as a simple rule of thumb, the three-year profit contribution they would be expected to make. Then divide the total cost of marketing and running your pipeline, including the sales conversations, by the number of signed-up customers, to get the average cost of acquisition. The ratio should show about a three to five times return.

> $100 spent on marketing should generate $300 to $500 in profit. If it generates less, your marketing isn't working well enough. If it generates more than this, you can afford to spend up on marketing and scale things some more, as you now know such expenditure is not a cost – it is a profit centre.

Summary

- Map out the journey you want and need to take your customers on, from becoming aware of you, through appreciating the value you offer, to trusting you, to considering buying from you – and doing it now.

- Experiment with a pathway until it works with refinements, or move on to other options.

- Measure each step, as well as the overall return on your marketing dollar, by the ratio of average customer acquisition cost over average lifetime value. If this is less than three, go back to improving your marketing method. If it's much more than five, it will pay you to spend more, as you have struck gold.

19
Sales Conversations

M any people say they hate selling. So, don't. Reframe what you're doing as providing diagnosis, education and service.

When selling doesn't work, it's often because the salesperson launches into telling their would-be customer the features and benefits; almost shoving them down their throat. This is like visiting a doctor who launches into prescribing medicine before hearing your problem and working out a diagnosis. First, understand if the client has a problem you can solve, how bad it is, what might have been tried before and what the consequences will be if it's not fixed.

Establish the customer's goals

A sales conversation must first establish the custom-er's goals, understand their challenges in achieving them and have the customer express their emotional frustrations and what they want as an outcome, *before* any discussion of what your product or service offers, how it solves their challenges and helps them achieve their goals.

CASE STUDY: TONY MCGINN

Fellow TEC chair Tony McGinn's first job was with a GM Holden car dealership in Ferntree Gully, a not-so salubrious suburb on the outskirts of Melbourne. The dealership didn't look like much, but it happened to sell more Holdens than any other dealership in Australia. As Tony found out, the reason seemed to be their system.

On his first day, Tony spoke to a family in the showroom and after a while was delighted to hear them say they wanted to buy a car. He proudly wrote up the sale documents and took them into the sales manager to authorise. To his surprise, the manager didn't seem too impressed. 'Did you follow the system I taught you to make the sale?' 'Well, no,' said Tony, 'but I've made the sale anyway.'

'Have you? Well, let's see what happens.'

When Tony returned to the sales floor to complete proceedings, he was mortified to find his buyers were having second thoughts and eventually walked away. No sale.

The manager's response was to tell Tony that if he ever failed to follow their system again, he would be sacked. A potential level nine screwup.

The key component that Tony had overlooked was to take prospective buyers for a drive, not in the new car but in their old car. While they were driving him around the block a few times, Tony was advised to ask them about their experience with the car. What did they like? What didn't they like? What was missing? What kind of use did they make of the car? Where did they drive and with whom? Had it been reliable, economical, fast enough, luxurious enough and so on?

Only then, armed with this information, was Tony to show them a car that would meet the needs and desires they had laid out for him. As he came to see, when that method was followed – when people could see a particular new car closely provided what they said they wanted in their own words – they bought.

Those insights, that stayed with Tony over the years in sales and his media business, he now passes on to other business owners around Australia.[94]

Presales positioning

Even in a car showroom, the customer is at least coming in with some implicit acknowledgement of the expertise of the salesperson. Of course, the more a customer accepts that you have authority in a field, the more likely they are to listen to and accept your advice. As we said initially, at the extreme end of this is the example of visiting a doctor where you generally accept their expertise, as well as granting them a considerable level of trust.

> The task of a salesperson is to have the customer perceive them as a trustworthy expert. The best way to achieve that is to be one. That means having a deep understanding in the domain of your customers' problems and honestly only recommending what will solve them.

If your product or service won't, then recommend someone else if you know they can. When you say to a customer, 'I don't think our product is right for you', what happens to the trust they have for you? They will likely take your word for anything else in the future and probably be so surprised, they'll talk about you with their friends.

If you ask most salespeople what their focus is on, they will often say it's about building relationships. No doubt there's an element of that, but failing salespeople can hide behind that when they seem unable to close a sale. They take being told no to heart and so don't risk anything. I'm not talking about pushy salesperson behaviour, but appropriately prodding a customer to act in their own best interests. To challenge them where necessary and being willing to be told no. The threat of being told no shouldn't derail their productivity.

You need your salespeople to be genuinely enthusiastic about your product or service. I realised this when I was working in the audiovisual production company in my early days, with my charismatic older partner. We would stand together in front of advertising agencies or company management and pitch to produce a show, using video, film, multiscreen slide projectors, singers, dancers, smoke machines and anything else we thought would make for a spectacular and effective launch for their new products. My partner exuded enthusiasm, while I was trying to be logical and careful I didn't say the wrong thing. Eventually, I came to understand his tone, body language and genuine belief that we could turn on an outstanding show was doing the selling far more effectively than anything I cautiously had to say.

Think of the last time you saw a fantastic new TV series on Netflix or somewhere else. Did you phone a friend, or next time you ran into them did you tell them how much you couldn't stop watching it, what a fabulous story it was, with great acting and how it kept you binge-watching until the end? That was selling in its finest form. Honestly passing on why you think someone would just love something and urging them to take it up. I'm betting you did it without holding back or feeling embarrassed.

If you or your salespeople can't express that level of enthusiasm about your product or service, stop selling it. Go back and make the product the complete and remarkable solution it needs to be, so you and your team want to tell people about it and want them to buy it. Because you believe, if they don't buy your product or service they'll be worse off without it.

Summary

- Don't launch into your features and benefits. Listen to what your customers want and their emotional frustration trying to get it with anything they've tried so far, before mentioning what you can do and why it will help them achieve their goals.

- Be a trustworthy authority who deeply understands the area and is willing to say you can't help if you can't.

- Enthusiastically tell people how they would love to use your product or service. If this is difficult, go back to improving the product until you can.

Conclusion

Building a company is, at the same time, one of the toughest and most rewarding things you can do. It'll take years of your life to do it and will challenge you in ways you can't foresee, but the journey is so worthwhile.

To bring a new business into existence and see it grow, you need to create a wonderful product or service. A complete and remarkable solution. One that's ten times as good as previous alternatives. To do that you first need to care about a niche of people and their situation. You must want to help them solve their problems and reach their dreams, by creating things they need as well as want.

You need to understand the value proposition they're looking for and how to communicate with impact. Then it's time to set your course for bigger things, laying out your vision, your mission, your strategy; and enrolling a committed team to take on the challenge.

You'll be working with your people, empowering them to be co-creators and take ownership, to play as a champion team for the sake of the mission, not just for themselves. You'll be striving to build a culture that nurtures them as individuals, while ensuring they live the values and purpose of the company. You'll want to become the employer of choice in your industry, so the right people want to work with you. These related challenges are probably the most demanding of any on your journey.

You must grow yourself in order to grow the company. Make the shift from expert to entrepreneur, from operator to owner. Be a leader. Give up being busy and become effective. Focus your time on strategic matters that move the needle.

Build the systems so the place can run without you. So new people know what to do and how to behave. Build a sales and marketing machine so that more lucky people can have their lives changed by interacting with you, with your team, with your products and services, with your brand.

Take care of the well-being of your team and yourself. Build a life as well as a business.

Those are the five springboards you need to break through your growth ceilings and make the quantum leap from Startup to Scaleup.

If there's a sixth springboard, it would be getting the right support. It can be lonely and frustrating trying to figure it all out and cope with the setbacks on your own. Get a mentor or a coach, join a network or a peer advisory group to work with you and shortcut your route to the top. The right mountain guide can make your adventure more successful and enjoyable, while helping to limit your screwups to the low-level, humorous in hindsight variety.

My mission is to help you build a bigger, *better* business, so you and others like you can build a better world. I hope this book has in some way empowered you on that journey.

Bon voyage.

Resources

Visit the website for further information on peer group and individual coaching: www.innovationconsult.com.au

Get a free Scaleup business plan: https://getreadytoscale.scoreapp.com

Follow Tom on social media for posts, articles and videos:

in www.linkedin.com/in/tomwilliamsinnovationconsult

f www.facebook.com/tomwilliamsbusinesscoach

Notes

1   Australian Government, *Small Business Counts December 2020*, www.asbfeo.gov.au/sites/default/files/2021-11/ASBFEO%20Small%20Business%20Counts%20Dec%20 2020%20v2_0.pdf, accessed 9 December 2022

2   Australian Bureau of Statistics, 'Counts of Australian Businesses, Including Entries and Exits' (25 August 2022) www.abs.gov.au/statistics/economy/business-indicators/ counts-australian-businesses-including-entries-and-exits/ latest-release, accessed 9 Dec 2022
    Duke, J, 'Spirit of enterprise alive and well despite high failure rate', *The Sydney Morning Herald* (24 August 2021) www.smh.com.au/politics/federal/half-of-australia-s-new-businesses-failed-to-survive-to-2021-20210824-p58leo. html, accessed 19 February 2023

3   The Nobel Prize, *Niels Bohr Biographical*, www.nobelprize. org/prizes/physics/1922/bohr/biographical, accessed 9 December 2022

4   *Ice Cold Murders*, www.amazon.com/Rocco-Schiavone/dp/ B07BLJB91B, accessed 14 December 2022

5   Grit, I, 'Everybody has a plan until they get punched in the mouth', Indy Grit Community (7 February 2019) https:// indygrit.community/blog/2019/2/9/everybody-has-

a-plan-until-they-get-punched-in-the-mouth, accessed
19 February 2023

6   Mitchell, S, 'The (not so) secret to JB Hi-Fi's success',
     Financial Review (14 February 2020), www.afr.com/
     companies/retail/the-not-so-secret-to-jb-hi-fi-s-success-
     20200212-p53zze, accessed 14 December 2022

7   Yong, D, Kobayashi, C, Da Costa, GS, et al., 'r-Process
     elements from magnetorotational hypernovae', *Nature* 595,
     223–226 (2021), https://doi.org/10.1038/s41586-021-03611-
     2, accessed 9 December 2022

8   UK Research and Innovation, 'Thank our exploding stars
     for our galaxy's gold' (7 July 2021), www.ukri.org/news/
     thank-exploding-stars-for-our-galaxys-gold, accessed
     9 December 2022

9   'The Apollo 11 LEVA moon helmet' (no date), https://
     apollo11space.com/the-apollo-11-leva-moon-helmet,
     accessed 19 February 2023

10   'The gold rushes of Victoria and California compared',
     Sovereign Hill Education Blog (15 October 2020),
     https://sovereignhilledblog.com/2020/10/15/the-gold-
     rushes-of-victoria-and-california-compared, accessed
     20 February 2023

11   Maslow, AH, 'A theory of human motivation', *Psychological
     Review*, 50/4 (1943), 370–396, https://doi.org/10.1037/
     h0054346, accessed 15 February 2023

12   Fairhurst, D, 'Harley Davidson is very clear about what
     it is selling to its customers – and it isn't motorcycles',
     HR (3 August 2011), www.hrmagazine.co.uk/content/
     features/harley-davidson-is-very-clear-about-what-it-is-
     selling-to-its-customers-and-it-isnt-motorcycles, accessed
     9 December 2022

13   Christensen, C, Cook, S and Hall, T, 'What customers want
     from your products', Harvard Business School (16 January
     2006), https://hbswk.hbs.edu/item/what-customers-
     want-from-your-products, accessed 20 February 2023

14   Connor, A, 'The dawn of the Japanese sport bike', Gear
     Patrol (22 December 2015), www.gearpatrol.com/cars/
     motorcycles/a170140/history-honda-cb750-universal-
     japanese-motorcycle, accessed 20 February 2023

15   Montes de Oca, B, 'Kodak invented the first digital
     camera (and shelved it)', *Slidebean* (1 May 2020), https://
     slidebean.com/story/first-kodak-digital-camera, accessed
     9 December 2022

16 Information from personal communication

17 McGovern, M, 'The ultimate guide to value propositions – with 39 examples you need now', *Resourceful Selling*, www.resourcefulselling.com/value-propositions, accessed 9 December 2022

18 Michel, S, 'The upside of falling flat', *Harvard Business Review* (April 2007), https://hbr.org/2007/04/the-upside-of-falling-flat, accessed 9 December 2022

19 Marshall, R, 'Investors say this cabana is cool', *Courier Mail* (1 April 2014), www.couriermail.com.au/news/queensland/sunshine-coast/business/investors-say-this-cabana-is-cool/news-story/4fca4846779a03a4fb1f15becf3d4e9b, accessed 9 December 2022

20 Ulwick, T, *Jobs To Be Done* (Idea Bite Press, 2016)

21 Marasco, C, 'Salbutamol', *Chemical & Engineering News*, https://pubsapp.acs.org/cen/coverstory/83/8325/8325salbutamol.html, accessed 8 February 2023

22 Drucker, P, *The Practice of Management* (1954, Harper & Brothers)

23 Petty G, Personal communication (2022)

24 Dry J, Recorded interview (2016)

25 Darwin C, *The Origin of Species* (John Murray, 1859)

26 Khan, O, 'The way forward: Balancing profits and purpose for business', *Avanade Insights* (21 April 2021) www.avanade.com/en/blogs/avanade-insights/responsible-business/balancing-profits-and-purpose-for-business, accessed 8 February 2023

27 Smith, A, *The Wealth of Nations* (W. Strahan and T. Cadell, 1776)

28 Denning, S, 'The origin of "the world's dumbest idea": Milton Friedman', *Forbes* (26 June 2013) www.forbes.com/sites/stevedenning/2013/06/26/the-origin-of-the-worlds-dumbest-idea-milton-friedman/?sh=18318707870e, accessed 9 December 2022

29 O'Brien, D, Main, A, Kounkel, S and Stephan, A, 'Purpose is everything: How brands that authentically lead with purpose are changing the nature of business today', *Deloitte* (15 October 2019) www2.deloitte.com/us/en/insights/topics/marketing-and-sales-operations/global-marketing-trends/2020/purpose-driven-companies.html, accessed 17 December 2002

30 Butler-Madden, C, 'How purpose led businesses are riding to the top', *Women's Agenda* (22 March 2022) https://

womensagenda.com.au/business/how-purpose-led-businesses-are-riding-to-the-top, accessed 17 December 2022

31   Landis, J, *The Blues Brothers* (Universal Studios, 1980)

32   *The Age*, 'A mission from God nears its end' (11 February 2003), www.theage.com.au/entertainment/movies/a-mission-from-god-nears-its-end-20030211-gdv7i1.html, accessed 22 January 2023

33   WiX Blog, '21 powerful mission statement examples that stood out' (21 May 2022), www.wix.com/blog/2020/12/mission-statement-examples, accessed 22 January 2023

34   Branson, R, *Virgin Rebel* (2013, Agate Publishing)

35   Christensen C, *The Innovator's Dilemma* (Harvard Business School Press, 1997)

36   Pereira, D, 'Southwest Airlines business model,' *The Business Model Analyst* (17 July 2022), https://businessmodelanalyst.com/southwest-airlines-business-model, accessed 8 February 2023

37   Kininmonth, C, 'The brave leadership of Sir Richard Branson', *The Growth Faculty* (9 June 2021), www.thegrowthfaculty.com/blog/richardbranson, accessed 21 December 2022

38   Conaghan, E, 'Small business trends 2023', Xero, www.xero.com/au/reports/business-trends, accessed 22 January 2023

39   Rosenbaum, E, 'As the Dow tanks, here is Warren Buffett on the biggest puzzle for investors: Intrinsic value of a stock', The Bottom Line, CNBC (5 December 2018), www.cnbc.com/2018/12/05/warren-buffett-on-the-biggest-puzzle-for-investors-intrinsic-value.html, accessed 26 February 2023

40   Blumenrath, S, 'The neuroscience of touch and pain', BrainFacts.org (3 February 2020), www.brainfacts.org/thinking-sensing-and-behaving/touch/2020/the-neuroscience-of-touch-and-pain-013020, accessed 21 December 2022

41   Dalio, R, 'How Ray Dalio built the world's biggest hedge fund', *Fortune* (13 September 2017), https://fortune.com/2017/09/13/ray-dalio-bridgewater-associates-book, accessed 26 February 2023

42   Green, M, 'Speech Acts', *Stanford Encyclopedia of Philosophy* (24 September 2020), https://plato.stanford.edu/entries/speech-acts, accessed 8 February 2023

43   The Predictive Index, www.predictiveindex.com, accessed
     26 February 2023

44   Gallup, *State of the Global Workplace 2022 Report: The
     voice of the world's employees* (2022) www.gallup.com/
     workplace/393623/state-global-workplace-report-2022.
     aspx, accessed 21 December 2022

45   Jackson, J, 'What's really suffering while working
     remotely? Collaboration and creativity', Lucidspark
     (17 September 2020) https://lucidspark.com/blog/
     remote-work-hurts-collaboration-and-creativity, accessed
     22 December 2022

46   Sky News, 'Company implements four day work week
     with "fantastic" results (20 February 2021), www.skynews.
     com.au/australia-news/company-implements-four-day-
     work-week-with-fantastic-results/video/4a91ea7e6ea99a29
     b09c59313d744268, accessed 8 February 2023

47   Atlassian, 'Company values', www.atlassian.com/
     company/values, accessed 8 February 2023

48   Schwarcz, J, 'Can one rotten apple really spoil the whole
     barrel?' McGill (3 December 2019), www.mcgill.ca/oss/
     article/nutrition-you-asked/can-one-rotten-apple-really-
     spoil-whole-barrel, accessed 22 December 2022

49   Lencioni, P, *The Five Dysfunctions of a Team: A leadership fable*
     (Jossey-Bass, 2002)

50   'Churchill and the Great Republic', The Library of Congress
     (no date), www.loc.gov/exhibits/churchill/wc-hour.html,
     accessed 26 February 2023

51   Library of Congress, *Respectfully Quoted: A Dictionary of
     Quotations* (2010, Dover Publications) p93

52   Pucie, C, 'Grand challenges in global health initiative
     selects 43 groundbreaking research projects for more than
     $436 million in funding', Bill & Melinda Gates Foundation
     (June 2005), www.gatesfoundation.org/ideas/media-
     center/press-releases/2005/06/funding-groundbreaking-
     research-projects, accessed 26 February 2023

53   Braithwaite, S, 'Zelensky refuses US offer to evacuate,
     saying "I need ammunition, not a ride"', CNN (26 February
     2022), https://edition.cnn.com/2022/02/26/europe/
     ukraine-zelensky-evacuation-intl/index.html, accessed
     26 February 2023

54   'Martin Luther King, Jr. I Have A Dream', American
     Rhetoric Top 100 Speeches (no date), www.

americanrhetoric.com/speeches/mlkihaveadream.htm, accessed 26 February 2023

55   Leslie, I, 'How Netflix changed the channel', Australian Financial Review (4 January 2021), www.afr.com/companies/media-and-marketing/how-netflix-changed-the-channel-20201211-p56mmz, accessed 26 February 2023

56   Krulwich, R, 'What is it about bees and hexagons?' NPR (14 May 2013) www.npr.org/sections/krulwich/2013/05/13/183704091/what-is-it-about-bees-and-hexagons, accessed 18 January 2023

57   Brian Cox, 'Why Do Bees Build Hexagonal Honeycombs?' *Forces of Nature with Brian Cox* (BBC, 27 June 2016), www.bbc.co.uk/programmes/p03zn0bp, accessed 23 January 2023

58   Napoli, L, 'The story of how McDonald's first got its start', *Smithsonian Magazine* (1 November 2016), www.smithsonianmag.com/history/story-how-mcdonalds-first-got-its-start-180960931, accessed 9 February 2023

59   Masters of Scale with Reid Hoffman, 'Why Culture Matters: Netflix's Reed Hastings' (20 January 2023) https://mastersofscale.com/reed-hastings-culture-shock, accessed 22 December 2022

60   'Ford installs first moving assembly line 1913', PBS (no date) www.pbs.org/wgbh/aso/databank/entries/dt13as.html, accessed 26 February 2023

61   Lohr, S, 'Making cars the Volvo way', *The New York Times* (23 June 1987) www.nytimes.com/1987/06/23/business/making-cars-the-volvo-way, accessed 22 December 2022

62   'Toyota Production System', Toyota (no date) https://global.toyota/en/company/vision-and-philosophy/production-system, accessed 26 February 2023

63   Peters, A, 'Inside Tesla's 100% renewable design for the Gigafactory', Fast Company (15 April 2019) www.fastcompany.com/90334858/inside-teslas-100-renewable-design-for-the-gigafactory, accessed 26 February 2023

64   Garan, Colonel R, *The Orbital Perspective: An astronaut's view* (2015, Metro Books)

65   Doerr, J, *Measure What Matters: How Google, Bono, and the Gates Foundation rock the world with OKRs* (Penguin Random House, 2018)

66   McChesney, C, Covey, S and Huling, J, *The 4 Disciplines of Execution: Achieving your wildly important goals* (Simon and Schuster, 2015)

67 Covey, S, *The 7 Habits of Highly Effective People* (Simon & Schuster, 2020)

68 Ogilvy, D, 'Business Heroes – David Ogilvy – The father of modern advertising', London Business School (1 March 2005) www.london.edu/think/business-heroes-david-ogilvy-the-father-of-modern-advertising, accessed 26 February 2023

69 Willuhn, I, Warnaar, P, Matos, J, et al., 'Striatal dopamine signals are region specific and temporally stable across action-sequence habit formation', *Current Biology* (7 February 2022), https://doi.org/10.1016/j.cub.2021.12.027, accessed 18 December 2022

70 Weinschenk, S, 'Shopping, dopamine and anticipation', *Psychology Today* (22 October 2015), www.psychologytoday.com/au/blog/brain-wise/201510/shopping-dopamine-and-anticipation, accessed 22 December 2022

71 Smittenaar, P, 'The good, the bad the dopamine', Hall & Partners, www.hallandpartners.com/thinking/culture/the-good-the-bad-the-dopamine, accessed 22 December 2022

72 Gilroy, R, 'Dopamine: It's a force of habit', *BioTechniques* (28 February 2022) www.biotechniques.com/neuroscience/dopamine-its-a-force-of-habit, accessed 22 December 2022

73 Clear, J, Atomic Habits (Penguin Random House, 2018)

74 Dr Dike, C, 'Stress vs. burnout – what's the difference', Doctor On Demand Blog (26 August 2022) https://doctorondemand.com/blog/mental-health/stress-vs-burnout, accessed 9 February 2023

75 Robinson, BE, 'The surprising difference between stress and burnout', *Psychology Today* (18 November 2020), www.psychologytoday.com/au/blog/the-right-mindset/202011/the-surprising-difference-between-stress-and-burnout, accessed 22 December 2022

76 Dalziel, AH, Maisey, AC, Magrath, RD, et al., 'Male lyrebirds create a complex acoustic illusion of a mobbing flock during courtship and copulation', *Current Biology* (10 May 2021), https://doi.org/10.1016/j.cub.2021.02.003, accessed 23 January 2023

77 Harley, A, 'Prospect theory and loss aversion: How users make decisions', Nielson Norman Group (19 June 2016), www.nngroup.com/articles/prospect-theory, accessed 22 December 2022

78 Psyblog, 'Loss aversion: The psychological bias against losses', www.spring.org.uk/2021/07/loss-aversion-bias. php, accessed 22 December 2022

79 Duffy, P, 'City Lore; Willie Sutton, Urbane Scoundrel', *The New York Times* (17 February 2002) www.nytimes. com/2002/02/17/nyregion/city-lore-willie-sutton-urbane-scoundrel.html, accessed 26 February 2023

80 Vaynerchuk, G, 'How to make 64 pieces of content in a day' (14 November 2019), https://garyvaynerchuk.com/ how-to-create-64-pieces-of-content-in-a-day, accessed 9 February 2023

81 'Elon Musk USC commencement speech | USC Marshall School of Business Undergraduate Commencement 2014, YouTube (17 May 2014), www.youtube.com/ watch?v=e7Qh-vwpYH8, accessed 27 February 2023

82 Rifkin, G, 'How Richard Branson works magic', strategy+business (1 October 1998) www.strategy-business. com/article/13416, accessed 27 February 2023

83 Chinn, A, 'Does BMW own Rolls-Royce?', The Car Investor (30 June 2022), https://thecarinvestor.com/does-bmw-own-rolls-royce, accessed 9 February 2023

84 Classic & Supercars, 'History of Bentley', https://classic-supercars.co.uk/history-of-bentley, accessed 9 February 2023

85 Trusted Brands Australia 2022, 'Bunnings Warehouse Award: Winner, Category: Australian iconic brand', www. trustedbrands.com.au/brand-showcase/bunnings, accessed 9 February 2023

86 Chung, F, 'Not as good as Bunnings', News.com. au (19 January 2016), www.news.com.au/finance/ business/retail/not-as-good-as-bunnings/news-story/b23138da9b6917f7af17b628d01818df, accessed 22 December 2022

87 McAdam, B, 'Still more profitable after customers flee your price rise', Profits Collective, https://profitscollective.com/ still-more-profitable-after-customers-flee-your-price-rise, accessed 22 December 2022

88 *The Guardian*, 'Saudi dove in the oil slick' (14 January 2001), www.theguardian.com/business/2001/jan/14/ globalrecession.oilandpetrol, accessed 9 February 2023

89 Chen, J, 'Veblen good: Definition, Examples, Difference from Giffen Good', *Investopedia* (18 January 2023), www. investopedia.com/terms/v/veblen-good.asp, accessed 19 December 2002

90   Your Brain on Money, 'How Apple and Nike have branded your brain', *Big Think*, https://bigthink.com/series/your-brain-on-money/how-apple-and-nike-have-branded-your-brain, accessed 22 December 2022

91   Platt, M, 'Cracking the code on brand growth', Knowledge at Wharton (7 January 2019), https://knowledge.wharton.upenn.edu/article/cracking-code-brand-growth, accessed 23 January 2023

92   Cialdini, RB, *Influence: The psychology of persuasion* (Harper Business, 2006)

93   Priestley, D, *Scorecard Marketing: The four-step playbook for getting better leads and bigger profits* (Rethink, 2022)

94   McGinn, T, Sales workshop and personal communication (2022)

Acknowledgements

I'd like to thank all my coaching clients, as they have been the proving ground for my ideas. They've shown me, via their feedback and their results, what works and what doesn't.

In particular, I want to thank Pippa Joseph, Hannah Chipkin, Michael Kent, Richard Evans, Toby Lawrence, Jesse Sharp, Lindsay Kotzman and Trinity Fitzgerald, who consented to me including elements of their stories in the book and provided feedback on an early draft. I also want to thank my colleague Glenn D'Costa for his support and feedback on a draft.

I want to thank Andrew Dick, Tony McGinn, Harvey Martin as well as other chairs in The Executive

Connection community for their contribution and encouragement.

I want to thank my partners in various businesses over the years, including Peter Attwood, Richard Graham, David Baillieu, Larisa Rudenko and Bob Borland. I want to thank business leaders I've interviewed, including Grant Petty and Justin Dry.

I want to thank Belinda Cabria for the illustrations and all the team at Rethink Press, including Bernadette Schwerdt, Lucy McCarraher, Eve Makepeace and Joe Gregory.

My parents gave me the freedom to follow my passions and passed on their own learnings about business from their personal and family experience. My children Kate, Jo, Beck and Michael have always supported me and my various endeavours.

I especially want to thank my wife, Joy, who as well as bringing her literary skills to bear in improving the book, has been a constant supporter and source of inspiration.

The Author

Tom Williams originally trained as a scientist before getting the entrepreneurial itch.

Over several decades, Tom has been the founder or co-founder of five diverse businesses, with exits including selling an investment management company to HSBC and taking a biotech from a Startup to a float on the Australian Stock Exchange.

Tom has also developed several innovations, including introducing video marketing for the pharmaceutical industry, the first mathematical model of the Australian stock market, the world's first business class for Qantas, and pioneering training for biomedical researchers to teach them how to commercialise their inventions. In recent years, he has focused on coaching expert-based business founders how to break through their growth ceilings and scale their businesses.

Tom has distilled everything he's learnt as a business owner and business coach into the formula spelt out in this book, for more growth with less stress. He believes anyone with passion can become an entrepreneur and business leader, once they understand the steps to follow.

For more information visit:

🌐 www.innovationconsult.com.au

❰f❱ www.facebook.com/tomwilliamsbusinesscoach

🔲 www.linkedin.com/in/tomwilliamsinnovationconsult

To get a free Scaleup plan visit:

🌐 https://getreadytoscale.scoreapp.com